I LOVE MONDAYS

Accomplish More, Make a Difference, and Create a Culture Shift

GEORGE ANASTASOPOULOS
DAKOTA LAMARRE

◆ FriesenPress

Suite 300 - 990 Fort St
Victoria, BC, V8V 3K2
Canada

www.friesenpress.com

Copyright © 2021 by George Anastasopoulos & Dakota LaMarre
First Edition — 2021

All rights reserved.

No part of this publication may be reproduced in any form, or by any means, electronic or mechanical, including photocopying, recording, or any information browsing, storage, or retrieval system, without permission in writing from FriesenPress.

All the Edward Hopper paintings referenced throughout the story were accessed digitally through www.edwardhopper.net, www.desmoinesartcenter.org, and www.whitney.org. Full citations of each painting can be found at their first appearances throughout the novel.

This is a work of fiction. Names, characters, business, events, and incidents are the products of the author's imagination. Any resemblance to actual persons, living or dead, or actual events is purely coincidental. The information and skills in the story are intended to serve as a general reference for understanding the underlying principles and practices of the subject matter covered. The opinions and ideas expressed herein are solely those of the authors. The authors are not engaged in rendering legal, managerial, or any other personal or professional advice or services in this publication. The strategies outlined in this book may not be suitable for every individual, and are not guaranteed or warrantied to produce any particular results.

The author, publisher, and their agents assume no responsibility for errors or omissions and expressly disclaim any responsibility for any liability, loss or risk, personal or otherwise, which is incurred as a consequence, directly or indirectly, of the use and application of any of the contents of this book.

Also avaliable as an audiobook.

All inquiries should be sent to:
Dakota LaMarre
inquiry@dakotalamarre.com
(905) 732-8754

ISBN
978-1-03-910976-6 (Hardcover)
978-1-03-910975-9 (Paperback)
978-1-03-910977-3 (eBook)

1. Business & Economics, Management
2. Business & Economics, Workplace Culture
3. Business & Economics, Leadership

Distributed to the trade by The Ingram Book Company

You are the solution.
TGIM!

TABLE OF CONTENTS

Introduction 1
Stage 1 — It's Just the Way It Is 6
1 — The Journey 7
2 — Floodgates 13
3 — Reflection 17
4 — It's a Mess 23
5 — Breakdown 29
Stage 2 — I Can Make a Difference 32
6 — Familiar Terrain 33
7 — An Unexpected Friend 39
8 — Child's Play 49
9 — Stories in My Head 55
10 — Authentically Human 65
11 — This Won't Work 73
12 — Finally, the Weekend 79
Stage 3 — I Am the Solution 86
13 — I Acknowledge You 87
14 — Parched Earth 95
15 — From the Top 101
16 — Confrontation 107
17 — Enrolling 115
Stage 4 — I Win Only When We All Win 122
18 — Pillow Talk 123
19 — Farewell for Now 129
20 — Requirements 137
21 — Fresh Start 145
Stage 5 — Great Leader, Great Human Being 150
22 — On the Other Side 151
23 — Welcome Home 159
Afterword 167
Acknowledgments 171

DEDICATION

*To every manager out there—
if you feel like you're sinking in quicksand,
here's a branch.*

INTRODUCTION

A note from George and Dakota:

We love Mondays.

That might seem odd, since many view Monday as the start of the workweek grind. It brings piles of affairs to deal with, problems to solve, a long to-do list, back-to-back meetings, and reports to prepare.

Then there are people and their "stuff"—emails, requests, and expectations.

You've likely heard co-workers complain that "everything's a priority" or "it's never been this crazy." Maybe you have thought the same.

We acknowledge you, our reader, for showing up to work every day, putting on a courageous mask, fighting the good fight, doing your best, trying to please everyone, and sacrificing yourself to do what's asked of you. Even though it might feel like it, you are not a victim.

Hierarchies and authority structures are found in your work, your family, charitable organizations, religious institutions, and government. This hierarchical world instills a belief system so subtly and early in life that we're not even aware it's happening. Our belief system guides what we do and what we think we can't or shouldn't do. This book isn't just about doing things differently. It is about embracing a fundamental shift in beliefs, from manager-thinking to leader-thinking, regardless of your place in the hierarchy. That shift can be life-changing.

This book provides practical and simple-to-apply skills to help you see your way out of the status quo.

This book is for you if any of this applies:
- You're done sacrificing your family and well-being for your career.
- You want to do great work and help others do the same.
- You're somewhere between fresh and seasoned, between rookie and veteran, working in any sized company.
- You're a wannabe manager but don't want to be like your manager.
- You're early in your career and won't wait to get to the top to create change.

GEORGE ANASTASOPOULOS

- You're a CEO or executive and are frustrated that your people don't take accountability, that your organization isn't proactive or innovative, and that everything falls on you.
- You're a business owner needing your lean team to work extraordinarily well together and be nimble and responsive to pivots and changes.
- You're interested in being a better leader, which is to say, a better human being interacting better with other human beings.

You can ditch the drudgery, frustration, and harmful health effects of "the way it is." You can (re)discover fulfillment in your work, appreciating that your job isn't just a means of making money. Your work should be a calling that ignites you and inspires you to make a difference.

Action is the answer, rather than complex plans and strategies. Action in the form of simple and transformative skills that you can start using right now to make a difference in your own life and the lives of others around you.

Our hero is not unusual. She takes the train into the city, works in a typical office environment, visits the art gallery, and has lunch with her co-workers. She's a talented, driven, committed employee and manager who's frustrated with the over-management culture. Her journey is one of enlightenment, enhancement, and transformation. It's about sage wisdom and the willingness to embrace it, about collaboration and co-creation.

DAKOTA LAMARRE

A Few Other Things

Though we wrote this book during the COVID-19 pandemic, we chose to depict a non-pandemic world. Whether you're reading this while working in isolation, in a hybrid model, or in your original at-work world, everything in this book still applies.

We know your time is valuable, so in this story, the pace at which our hero learns and adopts the presented skills is ambitious. With commitment and an open mind, the outcomes that she experiences are possible. This is a fable, which means we've used the fantastical to deliver our underlying messages.

We know that you are more than just a "business person," so we invite you to read this book as a human being. That's why we didn't write a typical business book, but rather a story with hopes, fears, and relationships. A story like yours.

Please, dive into the story and know that you are the narrator of your own. You have the power to make the rules and create lasting change.

• STAGE 1 •

IT'S JUST THE WAY IT IS

1

THE JOURNEY

No one likes to sleep on the train.

Jessica believed this firmly, though the man sitting across the aisle was trying his best to prove her wrong. A shiny spot formed at the corner of his mouth, signalling deep sleep.

Her fellow passengers shared the same zombified look, clad in business attire and up since the crack of dawn. The woman across from her held a thick report open in her hands but stared at the ground, gently rocking with the click-clack of the tracks.

Jessica wished she could have said goodbye to her daughter this morning. A peck on the cheek from her husband as she ran out the door was all the family time afforded her in the past twenty-four hours. On top of that, her team had little to show for Monday and Tuesday, like they were stuck on a treadmill, running ever faster but getting nowhere. The harder they worked, the less they seemed to accomplish.

Jessica had initially enjoyed the company's calm, collaborative, and creative culture. She and her co-workers operated in the blissful ignorance that comes from a growing market. She couldn't pinpoint when the change had occurred, but as their industry shrank, they stopped winning by default. Miscommunication and stress were now rampant. Priorities often conflicted.

The company's board was leaning heavily on the president, Gary. He responded to the increased scrutiny by steering even harder into his Ivy League management strategies, which included more reports, meetings, criticism, processes, and controls, overlooking the reality that people are responsible for execution.

Maureen, the vice-president of marketing and Jessica's boss, was a workhorse who made people feel guilty if they didn't sacrifice as much of their personal lives as she did. Nevertheless, Jessica respected the effort Maureen put into her work, especially considering few had expected her to succeed in this role.

Jessica used to love the idea of being in management, of having the opportunity to lead a great team and to empower other leaders through her work. Being promoted to director of digital marketing last year was a peak in her career, yet the valley that followed had come out of nowhere. Her intense passion and dedication finally paid off, but lately, she felt like she was leading her team astray, watching them descend further through stages of resignation to "this is just the way it is."

Resting her head against the cool window, Jessica watched the raindrops wiggle down the glass and thought about the past few decades. Her aptitude for marketing had shown early, as she helped her parents promote their small businesses. The business world offered the most promising career options, which, combined with her parents' pressure, convinced her to study marketing in university, even though her heart remained with her paintbrush.

Every elective she could spare had been in the arts. Something about art, mainly paintings, spoke to her and provided comfort. Art helped her tap into the rushing flow of creativity that ran deep within her. She took her art history professor's advice and toured Western Europe after graduating, visiting museums and art galleries until she ran out of money. Now, at thirty-six, she rarely visited galleries and hadn't picked up a paintbrush in years.

As if on cue, the train passed a billboard advertising the art gallery just a few blocks from her office. It was one of her favorite places in the city and housed some of her favorite artists' works, such as its collection of Edward Hopper paintings. The advertisement made Jessica think of the annual pass resting in her purse, collecting dust.

She caught her reflection in the cabin window.

"*What happened to you?*" The question rattled around inside her head.

Before she had stopped acting on her passion for art and fashion, she would show up to work each day dressed like a daring fashionista, her clothes echoing the intensity she brought to her work. Now, she was barely motivated to wear earrings.

Monday mornings once excited her, bringing new opportunities to leave her creative mark on the business world. Showing up early and leaving late most days, she had taken every chance to go above and beyond. This morning, Jessica found herself wondering what had changed. Monotony now devoured her creativity, as everything faded to gray—gray pantsuits, gray hairs, and gray skies.

The train came to a stop, gently jarring the passengers. The doors opened, and a flood of new commuters rushed to claim empty seats and avoid standing pressed against strangers. Someone was wearing too much cologne, making Jessica's eyes water.

From the outside, all seemed fine. She had a husband and a beautiful daughter, a lovely suburban home, and a high-paying job at a well-recognized large company. Somewhere along the way, the passion that fueled her had morphed into something else: a dull, sneaky sort of fear, manifesting in the form of doubt.

A culture of self-preservation and coping had enveloped her team, and each day the voice of doubt grew louder inside her head. It followed her home, like something foul she had tracked into the house on her shoe. It had crept into her relationship with Paul and Lily, at the dinner table and on weekends. She was a great provider, but lately, she wondered if she was a good parent and partner.

Her work seemed so purposeless. The tasks often didn't relate to the company's goals, and she was frustrated by the endless meetings and the obsession with quarterly results. She longed for an opportunity to drive change and make a difference for her team members, their customers, and her family.

She rarely challenged what was asked of her, stifling her inner genius. She did what she was told. She once had cherished a rushing flow of creativity, but it had dwindled to a trickling stream.

Over the past year, migraines had started to creep in, and recently they were accompanied by bouts of anxiety. Jessica knew she was fast approaching a breaking point, as surely as she knew her train would arrive at the station this morning.

She watched the usual turmoil on the platform as the train jolted to a stop. For a moment, as if reflected in the window, she had a vision of leading her colleagues to a better way of life, of empowering them to share their best ideas and helping them accomplish more in less time. She saw a world in which she created other leaders, who then took the culture of outstanding leadership viral. It was bigger than her, and it was beautiful.

The doors opened, spilling hundreds of people out into the city, all racing to their cages. The vision evaporated from her mind.

2
FLOODGATES

The elevator doors parted with a chime.

Jessica's workplace was quiet, but not calm. The air was thick with nervous energy. People darted to their cubicles in silence, like mice sneaking through a barn, fearing a cat.

Jessica made it to her office without acknowledging anyone. They were all focused on their computer screens, striving to look busy.

"*You ready for this?*" asked the voice in her head as she entered her password into her desktop.

"*Do I have a choice?*" she answered.

The floodgates opened as she started her applications, bringing emails and IMs with problems apparently only she could solve. Nearly a dozen messages were from Maureen, who had a habit of sending follow-up emails if she didn't hear back promptly.

In one thread, Maureen's first email was from 11:37 the night before, and the second at 7:16 this morning. The original read:

> Subject: Need this ASAP
>
> Jessica,
>
> Need a report on database errors from last quarter. Please send this to me by the end of day tomorrow.
>
> Thanks, Maureen

And the second email:

> Jessica,
>
> Reminding you to make this a top priority.

Jessica rolled her eyes. "This is a top priority," was Maureen's favorite expression. Jessica rubbed her temples, noticing the warning signs of a headache, when someone knocked at her door.

"Morning," Ravi said. "Got a minute?"

Ravi was an open book and her go-to guy. He loved to share his story about moving from India at the age of six, his family overcoming culture shock and language barriers to build a good life. Jessica promoted him to digital campaigns manager within a few months of her becoming director.

She envied the hope he exuded, his enthusiasm and desire not yet muted. Jessica wished she could save him from following in her footsteps.

"I had an idea last night that I want to share," he said, pushing his way through the door.

Jessica wished she could nurture Ravi's creativity, but the mere thought of new projects when she was continually trying to do more with less was exhausting. She knew it was only a matter of time before Ravi gave in to this exhaustion or quit.

"Let me catch up on some of this first," she jerked her head towards her computer.

The spark faded from Ravi's eyes.

"I'll try you later," he said, closing the door behind him.

She didn't have long to think about what life would be like without Ravi before her phone rang. It was Maureen, no doubt summoning Jessica to her office. This was how Jessica's day started several times a week. She let it ring and tried sifting through her inbox, triaging the most important requests, demands, follow-ups, and fixes.

The phone stopped ringing, ushering in a moment of silence, then lit up again. The display showed Maureen's extension, the little red bulb next to the phone line winking in mockery.

"That's enough," she said aloud, pushing herself from her desk and leaving the ringing phone behind. It was already time for a break.

3

REFLECTION

On her way to the break room, Jessica passed a meeting.

Through the conference room's glass wall, she saw one of her fellow directors standing at the front, lulling himself to sleep while delivering updates to his team. His staff was present in body but not in spirit. Some gazed into space, while others stared at their phones or laptops, "too busy" to offer their full attention. If someone were to paint a picture capturing the company's current work culture, this would be it.

The smell of freshly brewed coffee drew her into the break room, where she was surprised to see Gary, their president, filling a glass of water from the tap. He didn't hear her footsteps, and he was focused on something in his hand.

Jessica took two steps towards him, noticing the pill in his hand. He frowned, gently poked at the layer of belly fat stressing the lower buttons of his white, cotton dress shirt. He popped the pill into his mouth, turning around as he took a sip of water.

He froze.

"Jessica, hi," he said. "I didn't hear you come in."

"I didn't mean to sneak up on you," she replied, grabbing a coffee mug and filling it nearly to the brim.

"Yes, well," he said, clearly embarrassed. "I have to run to a meeting."

He nodded to her and left the break room carrying the glass of water.

The dark, spinning coffee in her cup was mesmerizing, and she found solace in its comforting aroma. She closed her eyes as she brought it to her nose and inhaled deeply.

She thought back to when she had met Gary years ago. He was the perfect image of a powerful executive. His movements conveyed the mindset that objects and people around him would bend to his will. If he were about to walk into a wall, he would expect the doorway to move to accommodate him.

He had also been a fun person to work with, back when favorable market conditions and a lack of healthy competition meant smoother sailing. You could often catch him in the break room, or he would stop by someone's desk to chat or share a laugh. Lately, it was hard to get him to crack a smile. His colleagues had given up trying.

Everyone knew the board was breathing down his neck and that the company had missed its targets for too many consecutive quarters. There was a running commentary around the office about when he would suffer a stress-induced heart attack. Never had Jessica met a man who carried so much on his shoulders. You could practically see it weighing him down.

A former Olympic swimming hopeful, he was no stranger to hard work, and he was used to being a lone wolf. Perhaps his greatest weakness was that he did not understand how to motivate people as a team where uncertainty, complexity, and ever-changing rules were commonplace. The youngest of four boys of a wealthy family, he had chosen to strike out independently and not join the family business like his brothers. His education had stuffed a lot of business theory into his head, yet his life experiences had done little to teach him to be a leader of people. Hard as he may micromanage, he couldn't get the machine to run as he wanted.

Jessica thought about this changed version of her company president as she sipped her coffee. Donning his usual tailored dark suit and bold tie, he still looked like his old self, albeit a little pudgier. Ninety-eight percent of him exuded confidence. It was only his eyes that ever betrayed him.

She had to admit that, while she didn't always agree with the way Gary ran things, she admired him for showing up to work every day no matter how bloodied he had gone home the night before. She felt sorry for him. She wished she could walk into his office and tell him he didn't have to control everything, that his people wanted desperately to do good work but needed his trust to do so.

"*Great advice*," she thought, reminded of her own tendency to micromanage. "*Maybe you should follow it yourself.*"

As she walked back to her office, her thoughts wandered to another important man in her life.

She had first met Paul at a friend's party, later learning that her friend had contrived much of the evening so the two of them would meet. Though she was adamantly focused on her career, meeting Paul had quickly made her reconsider her plans.

In previous dating attempts, some part of her had always needed to be sacrificed. It wouldn't be long into the relationship before she was either letting her passions fall by the wayside or felt guilty for working long hours. But everything had been different with Paul. He had accepted her exactly as she was from the beginning.

Their first date was at the art gallery. Paul was a gracious and engaged student as Jess talked him through some of her favorite paintings.

Soon after, they were spending almost every evening together, and Paul asked Jess to move into his downtown condo. It wasn't long before they were married, had a daughter, and moved to the suburbs.

Jess couldn't remember where the time had gone. Paul hadn't much changed, continuing to develop his career as a business writer and journalist from the comfort of an in-home office. He preferred working at home. When Jessica's promotion meant even longer hours at the office, Paul quickly took on more parent duty.

Paul was well-liked by his colleagues and by the people he interviewed. He was able to remain human and objective, even when the topics of conversation were unpleasant. He had a gift for translating peoples' complex thoughts into easily understood text. Jess envied him for his work–life balance.

In contrast, instead of her life stabilizing with the promotion, Jessica was putting in much longer hours. She often left the office after sundown. Paul assured her that he didn't mind picking up the slack around the house, but she knew that even he had a breaking point. His demeanor had been changing over the past few months. His patience wavered, and she couldn't blame him. She was less and less present, both physically and mentally, and there was no end in sight. She was tired of plastic-wrapped plates of leftovers from the dinners Paul and Lily had enjoyed without her. She sensed Paul was tiring of the arrangement.

Jessica sat down at her desk, once again ready to attack the mountain of reports, meeting invitations, and interruptions by her staff. She shivered, catching a sudden chill.

Something made the hair stand up on the back of her neck. She thought she heard a faint whisper from far away. It seemed to be trying to tell her that she could still be the leader she had always envisioned. She could create a culture that would reinvigorate her interactions with herself, her team, and her family.

Brushing it off as her imagination, Jessica shook her head and returned to attempt tackling her day of work. She would soon learn of forces conspiring to help her bring her visions to life.

4

IT'S A MESS

There was no escape from the electronic irritants.

Six new emails awaited, and the blinking light of a voicemail taunted her, undoubtedly from Maureen. Jessica pictured her boss sitting at her desk, frustrated that her go-to person for fixes, answers, and heavy lifting wasn't responding to her summons.

Scattered amongst the electronics and office supplies on Jessica's desk were tokens of her personal life that reminded her of home and why she worked so hard. To her left, she examined her degrees hanging on the wall.

"We want to reward your loyalty." She still remembered her previous boss sharing the good news, his oversized mustache nearly impeding his ability to speak. "We're going to cover a portion of your MBA."

Jessica was still grateful for the commitment her company had displayed in creating a path that had brought her to the director level. The phone number of a headhunter in her desk drawer made her feel like a traitor.

Her computer chimed to announce more emails. The sound had become a source of torment. The latest email apologized that the customer database was down. She knew how frustrating this would be to her team.

Checking her to-do list, she calculated the best way to manage her day. Many items had been carried over from the day before, and new tasks were piling up.

The list included follow-ups on initial requests, responses to requests from others, things to fix, meetings to attend, conflicts to resolve, and tasks to delegate. They all implied or demanded immediate attention. She felt as if her office floor had been replaced with quicksand that was threatening to swallow her.

Her phone rang again. She looked at the extension, winced, and picked up the handset.

"There you are," said Maureen. "Come to my office. Now, please."

"I... okay," Jessica replied.

It didn't matter what she was working on; Maureen wouldn't relent. Jessica put the phone back into its cradle; grabbed her notepad, pen, and cellphone; and stepped away from her desk for the second time that morning.

. . .

Jessica wondered if it were possible to die from too many meetings.

Before the growing competitive pressures threatened the company, Maureen had been one of Jessica's favorite co-workers. She was cuttingly brilliant and an expert decision-maker who had all the answers. As the situation worsened and Maureen was saddled with the interim vice-president responsibilities, she morphed into a micromanaging monster, stalking the halls seeking unsuspecting prey.

Jessica returned to her office after meeting with Maureen. She tossed her notebook on her desk and slumped into her chair, wondering how she would handle the added burden of running customer reports for Maureen.

Someone on her team could help, but Jessica would need to explain clearly to someone else what Maureen wanted. She would then need to follow up to ensure it would be done correctly and on time. It was simpler to do the work herself.

As she waited for her computer to come to life, her eyes found the picture of Paul, Lily, and herself on their last vacation to Greece. The photo was taken two years ago, and they hadn't had a proper getaway since.

A familiar feeling of guilt washed over her. She felt that she was letting her family down again. Though Paul loved his work, he put in a lot of hours and deserved to unplug. Also, the first five years of Lily's life had gone by in a flash.

Jess wanted her daughter to experience more of the world before she grew out of her sense of excitement and wonder.

Jessica didn't know how to get out of the vicious cycle that had trapped her. Time didn't care. It would carry on regardless of whether she found a way to enjoy life.

She still couldn't log into the customer database.

"Dammit," she said to herself. Through her open door, she could see that her team was struggling to manage the system failure. They were supposed to be launching another campaign today. Soon they would knock on her door and ask for instructions.

"Why do they always have to be told what to do?" asked the voice in her head. A migraine was fast approaching. She rubbed her temples. *"Why do I have to think like that?"*

She examined her to-do list, tapping her pen against the pad. Not knowing where to start, she rechecked her email, only to discover that the customer database would be down until tomorrow. Though it wasn't her fault, Jessica didn't relish telling Maureen this would delay her new campaign.

Another email from Ravi announced that a team member had called in sick, that he would do his best to pick up the slack, but that other priorities would be pushed back. Another email from the director of finance said that he needed Jessica's budget for the upcoming quarter by the end of tomorrow. The sinking feeling was back. The quicksand was creeping up to her waist.

She raised her coffee cup, took a sip, and nearly spit it out. It had grown cold waiting for her. She slammed it back down on the desk.

The sound of sirens accosted her ears. Maureen was calling her again. There was no way she could deal with another conversation.

As she reached for the handset, her hand collided with her coffee mug. In slow motion, Jessica watched as the cup toppled over, dumping dark liquid across her desk. She tried to push away but was too slow. Some of it dripped on her lap.

Leaping up, Jessica nearly choked as she swallowed the cold coffee. She reached for the box of tissues, spreading them across the growing brown puddle that now covered most of her desk. Her keyboard, mouse, notepad, phone, and work folders looked like the wreckage of a downed ship.

Her hands shaking, Jessica felt as if she were observing a scene of someone else's life. She felt dizzy. She was short-circuiting. The computer chimed again, eager to deliver the killing blow. It was from Maureen, and the subject line read, "Please come back to my office."

She felt like pushing her computer off the desk. Her head began to pound. She had to get out, now.

Not caring that she still held a soaking wad of tissues and wore a large coffee stain on her skirt, Jessica practically ran from her office. She needed to put as much distance between her and the situation as possible.

5

BREAKDOWN

Wiping tears from her cheeks, Jessica noticed a slight tremor in her hand.

"Come on. Stop!" Her voice echoed up the stairwell's concrete walls. It was tough to stop an anxious spell once it started. She was alone and scared, her heart pounding.

Head in her hands, elbows on her knees, she thought about the bottle of anti-anxiety medication that her doctor had prescribed for just such an occasion. She hated using it.

Knowing that focusing on the attack would only make it worse, she tried to think about things that would calm her down, pleading with her brain to let this pass.

Happy images of Paul and Lily came to mind. She thought of visits to her family's cottage when she was a young girl. Guilt followed. She hadn't visited the cottage in years. She recalled cooking herself dinner as a child and waiting for her parents to arrive home late from work.

She remembered many beautiful hours in front of her easel, followed by disappointment that she didn't paint anymore. Excitement over Lily's upcoming dance recital was pushed aside by a recollection of Lily's disappointment when Jessica had promised to be at one of Lily's soccer games but had failed to make it.

As the roller coaster finally came to a halt, Jessica's breathing slowed, and the fatigue set in. She felt like a ghost, and she knew she needed to bring herself back from the dead. As a young manager, she excelled at remaining positive and creative under stress. She needed that level-headed creativity right now.

She tried to open her mind to the possibility that she was missing something. There had to be other information out there, something she wasn't considering because her immediate surroundings had blinded her.

"I can't fix this on my own," she said aloud. "This is beyond me. I need someone to help me."

She was startled hearing herself declare out loud that she was overwhelmed. Equally startling, a voice seemed to whisper up the stairwell in response.

"Help is out there," it said. "Just ask."

Jessica had goosebumps.

Like fables from a forgotten age, Jessica recalled stories of companies where people loved to work. She longed to discover what they did differently and how they formed their culture. Perhaps she could create a new world for herself, her family, and her team.

She reminisced about the array of companies she studied during her MBA. From manufacturing to professional services, from pharmaceuticals to technology, she had learned that great culture has little to do with industry or economic climate and everything to do with people. Like a gentle swell of the sea, she felt a wave of hope rising to lift her upward.

"*Why not us?*" her inner voice asked, envisioning a future where she and her team could be the solution, and serve as an example of how to do things better.

Her episode over, her heart rate back to normal, she took a deep breath, smoothed her skirt, and left the stairwell. She wove her way through the rows of cubicles. Everything was the same, yet she saw the scene through a new lens. She was aware of something she wasn't able to perceive before, something she had learned to ignore. It was the possibility of once again loving her work, her life, and everyone in it.

Belief Shift: Resignation does not lead to inspired and extraordinary performance. "It's just the way it is" is a belief that indicates resignation (not to be confused with acceptance) to an unpleasant or undesirable situation. Hierarchy and authority structures are both implicit and explicit about how things are done, what's acceptable, what isn't, and how to fit into the existing culture. Read on to learn how you can make a difference.

DAKOTA LAMARRE

• STAGE 2 •

I CAN MAKE A DIFFERENCE

6

FAMILIAR TERRAIN

Jessica couldn't focus.

She had cleaned up the coffee spill as best she could, but was informed that the janitor was busy elsewhere and would deal with her office after lunch. The lingering sogginess made it hard to focus on her work.

The computer screen was blurry; her hands felt like someone else's. Something was tugging at her: the whisper she had either heard or sensed in the stairwell. It was like a soft breeze rustling the leaves of a tree.

Her emails might as well have been written in Greek. Another appeared in her inbox, this time from an unexpected sender. The art gallery was reminding her that it was almost time to renew her annual pass.

Jessica thought about how therapeutic it would be to roam the halls of the gallery. Visiting some of her favorite artwork might give her a chance to process this idea that she could create change within her team, that maybe there was someone out there who could help her.

She made the judgment call to take an early lunch.

She barely noticed the people she passed as she rode the elevator to the lobby and stepped out into the city streets. Her mind raced with questions as she walked.

Did she have to suffer the fate of late nights and pointless meetings? Did she have to observe helplessly as her work schedule continued to build animosity in her husband and daughter? Did she have to watch her bosses be miserable and her team members slowly descend towards the same fate? Or could things be different?

Whatever hope that still flickered within her was making a final effort to claim her attention. She wasn't sure how it would be possible, but she knew, as sure as she knew her name, that it was.

The large door creaked as she pushed it open.

"Ticket please," said a man in a red jacket.

Jessica rummaged through her purse for her pass.

Inside the quiet, cool gallery, she retraced the path she took on her first date with Paul. Ten steps in was where he admitted to knowing nothing about art. Twelve steps in was where she forgave him. Down the hallway to the right was where he asked her if she wanted kids. A bold move on a first date, and yet, she felt comfortable saying yes. She knew he could be the someone special she almost gave up hope of finding.

She reminisced about this younger version of herself, chuckling as she flashed back to Paul struggling to comprehend the paintings he examined. She wished she could reach through time and take young Jess by the shoulders, to shake her and tell her to prioritize what's important. She feared it was too late.

A year and a half after their first date, Paul proposed. A year later, she was pregnant with Lily, an unexpected gift. They hadn't planned on having children so soon. They had shared tears of joy when Jess walked out of the bathroom with a bashful smile and a positive pregnancy test in her hand.

Lily had already grown into such a vibrant little person. It was a joy for the two of them to bear witness as she explored the world with reckless abandon. They had started talking about having another child not long after Lily was born, Paul practically begging to expand on their little family. Given her circumstances, the thought of bringing another child into her unbalanced life scared Jessica.

"I don't believe in myself," she said to Paul sometime last year. "It's not that I don't believe in you, or even in us. I just don't feel like I can take on anything else right now. It wouldn't be fair to you, or Lily, or the new baby."

After that conversation, Paul dropped the subject entirely. Jess was afraid he had given up hope.

DAKOTA LAMARRE

As she entered the wing of the Edward Hopper collection, a sense of urgency drew her forward. The voice that had drawn her here seemed to be coming from down the hall. Despite her curiosity at what waited ahead, she couldn't help but smile at the memory of introducing Paul to Hopper's work.

He didn't get it at first, but she pointed out how well Hopper captured Western culture. His paintings often featured solitary people staring off at some point far on the horizon. Jess loved Hopper's work. The simplicity and implied loneliness resonated with her.

As she walked along the rows of paintings, passing the framed snapshots of a woman gazing out of a window, a scene at a bar, a woman sitting alone at a table, Jessica's eyes welled. She was struck by a wave of gratitude, for her amazing family, and for the life she worked so hard to build. She worried that another bout of tears was on the way. Thankfully, no one else was in the room.

She looked up at one of her favorite paintings, *Compartment C, Car 293*[1]. It depicted a woman sitting alone against a train compartment's green background, and it reminded her of herself.

Her family was who she was working for, along with the urge to keep others from falling into the same trap she had. She was ready to act, believing that things could be different,

---

[1] Edward Hopper, Compartment C, Car 293, 1938, https://edwardhopper.net/compartment-c-car.jsp, accessed 23 March 2021.

that she could build a culture where she didn't feel like a hostage in her own office. She didn't yet know how to make it happen, but she could picture a team of strong people who were self-sufficient and confident in their abilities, and who were capable leaders guiding their teams to victory.

The question wasn't what she needed to learn, but who she could ask for help. Racking her brain, no one came to mind. She was still alone.

The tension in her shoulders and pressure between her temples had abated. She was soothed by her favorite artworks. Though her problems were far from solved, she at least felt better. With nothing but hope for a brighter future, she braced herself to head back to the office.

She glanced up at the woman in the painting.

"Can you help me?" she jokingly asked.

She stood up, turning towards the exit. "Maybe I'm crazy," she muttered. "I can't be the one to make change. At least, not alone."

She almost toppled backwards over the bench as a voice announced, "You're not crazy. And you're not alone."

7
AN UNEXPECTED FRIEND

Jessica whipped around, looking for the source of the voice.

"Who said that?" she asked.

"Over here," the voice came from near the wall.

She crept slowly forward.

"What's the matter? Are you afraid?"

The voice was coming from the painting of the woman sitting on the train.

"What the…"

Jessica knew it had to be a trick of the acoustics. This painting couldn't be talking to her.

"A little closer," the painting said.

She hopped back, her hands held up as if to protect herself from an oncoming blow.

"That's not possible," she said.

"Isn't it?"

Checking up and down the hallway, Jessica made sure there was no one around. The woman in the painting lifted her head, revealing a pair of deep blue eyes under the brim of her hat. She winked at Jessica before looking back down at the book on her lap.

Jessica rubbed at her eyes, blinking heavily, and watched as the woman turned a page.

"What's going on?" she demanded. "What are you?"

The woman in the painting lifted her head again.

"I go by many names," she replied.

Her voice was the same one that had called to Jessica in the stairwell earlier.

"So, you're... what?"

"I'm a friend," the woman said. "I'm here to partner with you on this journey if you're willing to let me."

Her eyes fell back down to her book as she flipped a page and scanned it casually. She spoke as if there was nothing out of the ordinary about a talking painting.

"*What is going on?*" asked the voice in Jessica's head. She was ready to walk away, to wash her hands of this nonsense. She wondered if she should look into seeing a psychiatrist.

"I'm sorry," Jessica said, leaning closer, "Why are you talking to me? And why are you in a painting?"

The woman closed the book and placed it on the seat next to her, folding her hands and resting them on her crossed legs, offering Jessica her full attention.

"I see I've piqued your curiosity," she said. "I'm talking to you because you reached a pivotal moment earlier today when you experienced a belief shift and realized that you don't have to accept things the way they are at your company. When you admitted to yourself out loud that you couldn't do it alone, and you asked for help, you awakened me."

The woman in the painting smiled and continued, "And I'm in this painting because I always present myself to those who ask for help in a way that resonates with them. In this case, through the works of one of your favorite artists."

The woman spread her hands, gesturing to the edges of the painting that contained her.

"As I whispered to you earlier," the woman continued. "Help is out there; you just have to ask."

"So, you're here to help me fix my company?" Jessica asked.

"I wouldn't say fix, Jessica. It implies that something is broken."

"How else would you describe it?"

"How would you?"

Jessica thought about it, then sighed heavily.

"It's fine."

"So, you weren't crying in a stairwell earlier today?"

There was no hostility or accusation in the woman's voice, but the words landed.

"Okay, things are bad," Jessica sighed.

"When was the last time they were good?"

Jessica was at a loss for words. Thinking back through the past year, she realized that she and her team were trapped on a spectrum between "just okay" and "downright awful."

"No matter what we do, we can't get ahead. We're so busy fixing problems that we don't think strategically. It doesn't matter how much we do. The pile of urgent tasks gets bigger every day. It's like we're blindfolded and running at full speed, probably towards a brick wall. I know we need a new approach, but I don't know where to start. And I don't even know who to blame for why we're here in the first place. Do I have to take it the way it is?"

Jessica had finished speaking, but the woman in the painting wasn't eager to fill the silence. She watched as Jessica uncomfortably dealt with the weight resting on her shoulders.

"I'm here with you," was all the woman said.

Jessica felt exhausted. She knew she wouldn't break down as she had before. The woman in the painting's presence brought her peace.

"So, what to do about it?" the woman asked.

Jessica wished more than anything that she had an answer. Her head drooped low.

"What are you experiencing right now?"

"I'm tired, afraid, lonely," Jessica said. "I feel like I've trapped myself in this situation, and I'm powerless to get out of it."

"You sound like me," the woman replied. "Here on the train, surrounded by people, yet choosing to sit alone."

Jessica could relate.

"What do I do?" she asked. "I can see some of the problems, but I don't feel like it's my place to fix them."

"Whose place is it?"

"It has to come from the top, doesn't it?"

"Does it?"

"I don't make the rules," Jessica said.

"Who does?"

The challenge was without blame or hostility.

"*Maybe it doesn't have to be the way it is,*" said the voice inside her head.

"How does a video go viral, Jessica?"

The sudden tangent caught Jessica off-guard.

"People see it, love it, and share it?"

"Are you asking?"

"I'm telling," Jessica said. "But what does that have to do with our company?"

"Does an idea spread any differently?"

Jessica's immediate reaction was to argue, but she found herself unable to refute the woman's claim.

"You're saying that change can come from anywhere? That even I can make it happen from where I am, in my company's middle management?"

"What do you think, Jessica?"

"I guess so, hypothetically. But I can't do it alone."

"Are you alone?"

"Not fully. I have a few good people on my team."

"Do you trust them?" the woman asked.

"Of course I do, they're…" Jessica trailed off, sensing that she couldn't get away with a shallow answer and that she needed to peel back a few more layers to reveal a deeper truth. "I do trust them, in a way. I trust that they have the right intentions, the right motivations behind their actions, that they're good people. On a deeper level, when I think back to how things have gone in the past when we've come up short as a team, I don't fully trust their commitment to each other."

Sharing this with the woman in the painting was the first time Jessica had been able to articulate it fully to herself. She experienced a release of pressure, less weight on her shoulders.

"Thank you for sharing," responded the woman. "I acknowledge your courage in admitting that. It took a lot of honesty and integrity to reveal that part of yourself."

"But so what?" Jessica said. "Knowing doesn't help. Trust takes so long to build, and it's so easy to lose."

"I would like to propose that trust is the easiest, most human thing you can create with someone. It's child's play."

"I don't buy it."

"Are you at least browsing?"

Jessica frowned, confused.

"Where are you on the spectrum from open-minded to closed-minded?"

"I can be skeptical," Jessica said.

The woman in the painting chuckled.

"Alright, Sally Skeptic, you have a daughter, yes?"

"Lily," Jessica nodded.

"When Lily comes home from school, ecstatic because she got a good grade or because she made a new friend, do you not celebrate with her?"

"Of course. We let her pick what she wants to have for a special treat, and we spend quality time together as a family to anchor the occasion. It helps keep her motivated to keep trying. We used to do it all the time before I started staying late at work. Now I think she and Paul often celebrate without me."

"I see," the woman in the painting said, letting Jessica get lost in the reverie of days past and the sadness of days present. "And, when Lily's dreams don't come true, when she gets a bad grade or a classmate is mean, do you not sit with her in her sorrow and love her unconditionally? And do you not always support, encourage, and equip her?"

"What does how I raise my daughter have to do with the issues facing my team?"

"Why are you saving all your love, humanity, compassion only for your family?"

The woman watched the gears turning behind Jessica's eyes.

"We're all just people, Jessica," she continued. "If you expect your people to leave their humanity aside as soon as they enter the office, it's going to tear them in two. We're all kids on a playground wanting to be loved, celebrated, and acknowledged."

Jessica was amazed. It was so simple, so obvious, and yet, so rare in the business world.

"Try this approach with your colleagues and watch how quickly your relationships with them change, how quickly you establish trust. You hire people for their abilities, correct? You seek to bring people into your company that are smart, capable, creative?"

"Of course."

"Then trust and empower them to be the smart, capable, creative people that they are. Then acknowledge and celebrate their greatness with them. Can you do that?"

"I can."

"Are you totally enrolled?"

"I'm sold."

"I asked if you're enrolled."

"What's the difference?"

"Enrolled means you've embraced the idea as yours because it's sensorial, aspirational, and emotional. It's something you can picture as real because it's impacted your senses, you believe it's something worth striving for, and it's touched your emotions," said the woman. "You must picture it, feel it, and want it more than anything. If we're going to work on this together, you must commit to making it happen."

"Okay," Jessica said, her vision of a better team culture returning, followed by a burning desire to make it come true. "I'll do it."

"When?"

"I don't know," Jessica averted her gaze.

"When is the best time to plant a tree?"

"What?"

"20 years ago," the woman answered from her train compartment. "When's the next best time to plant a tree?"

Jessica caught on.

"Today," she answered.

"Nothing will change until you take action."

"I get it," said Jessica. "I'll do it."

"Come back when you have, and we'll debrief and move on to the next skill."

In the painting, the woman grabbed the book from the bench next to her, opened it, and began again to read in silence. The conversation was over.

Jessica's footsteps echoed as she made her way to the exit. She considered how strange her experience had been and the new hope it had inspired within her.

"*This can't be real,*" said the voice in her head. "*I must be imagining things or talking to myself. Or I've finally gone off the deep end...*"

She felt she was in a strange fictional world where paintings could talk and dreams could come true. Art had always spoken to her, but this was a bit much. She wondered if it was real or just her imagination.

"*Imagination or not, I'm going to make it real.*"

DAKOTA LAMARRE

8

CHILD'S PLAY

The rest of the afternoon ran away from her.

The office's demands sucked her in, one fire after another demanding immediate attention. She barely had the headspace to think about the tasks at hand, let alone her assignment from the woman in the painting. Away from the gallery and the painting's encouragement, it was easy to ignore her homework and succumb to the office's chaos.

The train ride home was much the same as the morning. Men and women in wrinkled clothes slumped in the seats, eyes glossed over, exchanging yawns. The train pumped them away, like an artery, from the heart of the city. However,

Jessica wasn't yawning. She tried to make sense of the emotional roller coaster of a day.

Jessica hoped to do some work at home that evening, but it didn't happen. She felt too exhausted. The reports and emails would have to wait another day.

The next morning in the office was quiet compared to the day before. It was shaping up to be a "just okay" day. The manageable busyness was drowning out any straggling thoughts of trust and team building. She blocked off the afternoon in her calendar to catch up on quarterly reports.

Lunchtime arrived. Jessica walked to the break room to retrieve a Caesar salad she had put in the fridge. She hoped to sneak in a few extra minutes of work as she ate at her desk. She nearly collided with Ravi as she rounded the corner into the bullpen.

"Boss, there you are," he said, excited but hesitant. "We came out ahead of projections on last month's campaign. Way ahead. I have the metrics and want to share them with you."

Their team's results had been underwhelming over the past few months, but Ravi's idea to re-segment customer data to create highly targeted campaigns had worked. She scanned the data on the report he handed her.

"That's great," Jessica said. "Good work."

She was about to brush past him when she heard a voice in her head.

"*Nothing will change until you take action.*"

"*Until I take action...*" she said to herself.

Thinking of Lily, she saw Ravi with her heart instead of her head, as a real human being instead of a piece of machinery that produces outcomes. Why not right now? Ravi was already walking away, a little bounce in his step because of his small victory.

"Hey," Jessica called, causing him to turn around. "What are your plans for lunch? Let's go out for a bite to celebrate."

It was as if Jessica had told him a poodle had taken Gary's place as president of the company. Ravi was baffled by her suggestion. His brain froze as he tried to compute.

"I thought you were busy the rest of the day," he said.

"It can wait. This is more important."

The conviction in her voice made the invitation impossible to refuse.

"Okay," Ravi said, smiling broadly.

"Meet me at the elevators in five minutes?" she said. "I have to take care of something."

Depositing her salad back into the fridge, Jessica psyched herself up. Hurrying through the corridors of cubicles, she approached the corner office as Maureen was exiting, her arms laden with her laptop and note-taking supplies.

Maureen had a quick wit and always knew what she was talking about, yet people usually remembered her for her frown.

"Maureen," Jessica said. "Ravi crushed it with last month's campaigns. We're going out for lunch to celebrate. Would you like to join us?"

Jessica might as well have been speaking Klingon.

"No," Maureen replied. "I have a meeting with Gary."

Jessica's excitement deflated as Maureen took a step away from her.

"Are you sure you have time for a long lunch?" Maureen spoke over her shoulder.

"I'll make time," Jessica said, her hands on her hips. "This is important."

"I still need those customer reports by the end of today. Make it a priority."

The accusation in her voice stung, as if Jessica had already come up short. Maureen didn't stick around long enough for Jessica to issue a spicy retort, not that it would have done any good.

Frowning, Jessica tried to shake off this distasteful interaction as she made her way towards the elevators.

...

The pair wiped tears of laughter from their eyes as they stepped off the elevator.

They had reveled in Ravi's victory and contributions to the team as they enjoyed California rolls at the sushi bar across the street. Arriving back at the office, they looked like two old pals who had finally reconnected after a long time apart.

At her desk, Jessica felt better than she had all week. The remaining tasks on her list felt manageable, even a little exciting.

Towards the end of their lunch, Ravi had asked Jessica if he could take a run at the quarterly reports, eager to sink his teeth into something meaningful and new. She had agreed, knowing that she would have to review his work, but happy to offer him the opportunity to learn. It also meant she could work on Maureen's customer reports and the team budget for the director of finance.

Jessica was in awe of the chain reaction from the newly established trust between her and Ravi. It presented an opportunity for him to take on a new challenge, and an item in her calendar had simply vanished. Compared to her previous attempts at delegating, today had flowed naturally. She found herself wondering if it could always be this simple.

She saw Ravi in a new light. He was more than an employee; he was a person who wanted to learn, win, and celebrate his accomplishments.

What still bothered Jessica was the continued impasse with Maureen. Maybe she had expected this exercise to work wonders instantly, and coming up short with her boss left her feeling shortchanged.

She sent the budgets to the finance department, and the customer reports to Maureen. As she added her final edits to Ravi's report, she glanced at the clock. It was only five-thirty, and she was almost done for the day.

"Hooray for small miracles," said the voice in her head.

Considering how late she usually arrived home, she doubted Paul and Lily would notice if she made an extra stop before hopping on the train. She experienced a twinge of guilt at not taking the opportunity to head home early, but she was excited to get back to the art gallery to share her achievements with her new friend and learn about what came next. She also wanted to prove to herself that her conversation yesterday hadn't just been in her imagination.

9

STORIES IN MY HEAD

Jessica checked up and down the hallway before creeping close to the painting of the woman on the train. They were alone.

"Well," she said. "I did it."

"And?"

The woman in the painting didn't stir, like she couldn't hear anything at all. Jessica frowned at *Compartment C, Car 293*, wondering whose voice she had heard.

"Over here," it called again, accompanied by the first notes of Beethoven's "Für Elise."

Jessica took a step back, searching Hopper's works for someone near a piano. A few paces to her right, she found what she was looking for, a painting of a man and a woman named *Room in New York*[2]. The man sat in an oversized stuffed chair reading a newspaper while a woman in a red dress fiddled with a piano.

"You've changed paintings?" Jessica asked.

"I thought it was appropriate," the woman said, letting the notes fade to silence and turning towards Jessica. "Tell me more."

"I used your skill with Ravi," Jessica said. "We connected as people. Work wasn't the dominating factor in our relationship. He even volunteered to take a task off of my plate. Can you imagine? It was like, being human with a member of my team made one of my problems evaporate."

Jessica paused, looking down at her shoes.

"May I call you Jess?" asked the woman in the painting.

Jess nodded.

"Jess, what aren't you telling me?" asked the woman in red.

"I invited Maureen to join us," Jess replied. "She spit in my face."

"Not literally, I hope," the woman said. "I sense you think Maureen was wrong to decline your invitation?"

"That's right," Jess replied.

"How is this opinion serving you?"

"It's not," Jess laughed half-heartedly. "But I've been known to have strong opinions."

---

[2] Edward Hopper, *Room in New York*, 1932, https://edwardhopper.net/room-in-new-york.jsp, accessed 23 March 2021.

"That's something we can work on," the woman said. "I acknowledge you for completing this exercise with Ravi and Maureen, despite the different outcomes. What was the impact of that?"

"I could see it in Ravi's eyes," Jess glowed. "The excitement and eagerness to learn. He was like a little kid on a field trip."

"And the impact on you?"

Wrapped up in her improved relationship with Ravi, Jess hadn't thought about the impact of her actions on herself.

"I got a major task off my plate."

"Anything else?"

"It felt good to be human," she said. "It's light and airy. I'm doing what I'm supposed to be doing."

"And what's the larger impact?"

"I want to spread this power, the idea that we can accomplish more by doing less. I empowered someone on our team to make a difference. I want to use this thinking to change the way our team operates, and I want it to go viral, to get others on board, spreading this idea to the people around them."

"You want to share this with everybody?"

Jess nodded.

"Even Maureen?"

The tightness in Jessica's chest and shoulders returned.

"What are you experiencing?"

"I feel cheated," Jess sighed. "I hoped that Maureen would join us and that I could start making progress in our relationship. I tried not to let it affect my lunch with Ravi, and I think I succeeded, but it still sucked."

DAKOTA LAMARRE

The woman in the painting looked longingly at the man reading the paper, as if she wished he would speak to her.

"We cannot control the way others react to the things we do and say," she said. "We can only control the way we react to their reactions."

Jess raised an eyebrow.

"Say that again, please."

The woman turned back to her.

"We cannot hope to control anyone else's thoughts or emotions, only our own. I have no control over whether you decide to listen to what I'm saying or how you interpret the things you hear. That's the uncertain thing about communication. If the listener decides to take something you say or do personally, that's up to them. You have the power to choose how you react to their response. You can choose whether to take their reaction personally."

Jess crossed her arms in disbelief.

"I see that Sally Skeptic is back," the woman chuckled. "Okay, Jessica, describe your relationships with your closest co-workers. Let's start with your boss."

"I thought we were going to go over the next skill," Jess said.

The woman in the painting slowly turned back towards the piano.

"Okay, wait," Jess held up her hand. "My relationship with Maureen isn't great. I don't agree with the way she runs the team. I have a lot of respect for the amount of work she does, but I don't like that she expects the same from everyone else. And I don't think she's a good communicator."

"You took it personally when she said she didn't want to join the two of you for lunch," the woman said. It wasn't a question.

"Of course I did. She…" Jess paused.

"What are you becoming aware of?"

"That I've made up her side of the story. I don't know what Maureen thought when she declined my invite."

"What's the impact of that story on you?"

"I want to have a good relationship with my boss, and her rejecting me made it seem like that wouldn't ever be possible, like she was saying that having a relationship with me isn't worth her time."

"Did she actually say that?"

Jessica realized how difficult it had been to control her reaction to Maureen. Jess wondered how often she made up stories for other people in her life. She winced and looked down.

"I'm here with you," the woman in the painting said.

"I'm sorry," Jess replied. "I didn't realize that this was so important to me."

"No apologies necessary," the woman waited for Jessica to become present again. "Sounds like you're a human being. What's opening up for you right now?"

"I'm seeing our interaction differently. The look on Maureen's face when she said she had a meeting with Gary,

I feel like it's the same look I have on my face when she summons me."

"What does that mean to you, being able to see your boss's perspective?"

"I want to help her not feel like that anymore. I know I hate that feeling of dread. I miss the days when I was excited to go visit my boss."

The woman in the painting smiled and nodded.

"What will you do with what you now know?

"I'm going to stop making up stories in my head about what Maureen is thinking and feeling," Jess said. "And try to be more conscious of other areas in my life where I'm making up stories for other people."

Jess took a deep breath, surprised by how much better she felt.

"Should we close this chapter on Maureen and move on?" the woman asked.

"Yes. Can we talk about Ravi now?" Jess answered.

"How is your relationship with him?"

"It should be great…" Jess trailed off.

"But?"

"My relationship with him brings me nearly as much stress as my relationship with Maureen," Jess sighed. "He's one of my favorite people, but he's constantly coming up with new ideas or new ways to do things."

"Sounds like that should be a good thing."

"It should be," Jess agreed. "But because we're so bogged down in the urgent day-to-day work, it ends up being exhausting. I think today's lunch helped with our relationship."

"How so?"

"It allowed me to see his passion for learning and trying new things as a strength, instead of something to be managed. It helped us to co-create an opportunity for him to act on that part of his personality."

The woman smiled at Jess.

"What?" Jess asked.

"I'm just smiling," she said. "What did you learn?"

"That empowerment really is easy, isn't it?"

"Are you asking?"

"No," Jess said, hands on her hips. "I'm telling."

"Let's talk about relationships," the woman continued. "More importantly, how we connect with people we have relationships with."

Jess shifted closer.

"Every relationship we have, whether personal, professional, or with a non-human entity like a company, will experience some or all of three distinct stages. The first I call passion. I'm sure you experienced this when you first started dating Paul or got your promotion. In this stage, everything is perfect. You're excited to think about that person or thing. It's the honeymoon phase. There's only one problem."

"It never lasts," Jess said.

"Exactly," said the woman. "Eventually, something comes along to shatter this illusion of perfection. You realize that your new partner leaves the cap off the toothpaste, that your boss has bad breath, that the office coffee tastes like dirt. Once you notice one flaw, more and more emerge. How could you have been so ignorant? It's a disaster! I call this phase 'warts.'"

"Warts," Jess chuckled. "And once you see them, you can never unsee them until the passion is gone forever."

"You can't go backward," the woman agreed. "And if you don't go forward, you'll be stuck forever. This is why people leave companies and bosses, or they disengage to the point that they might as well not even be there. This is also where most romantic relationships fail. They don't move past the warts stage."

The woman looked longingly at her partner across the table, sighing softly.

"Sounds like that's where I'm stuck with some of my co-workers," Jess said, pulling the woman's attention back. "What's the third stage?"

"What do you think it is?"

Jess scrolled through early memories of Paul, first noticing his faults, then coming to accept them.

"Appreciating the good and the bad," Jess said. "Accepting the person for who they are, loving them despite their flaws."

"Acceptance," the woman nodded.

"How do I get there?"

"Just as we're all kids on a playground who want to be loved, celebrated, and acknowledged, we're all individuals with unique perspectives. Attachment to your perspective creates separation. Openness to another creates opportunity."

"Yes, but it's much easier said than done to stop taking things personally," Jess said. "How do I stop my thoughts and opinions from hijacking my conversations and relationships?"

"Can you silence that little voice in your head that just argued with me?" said the woman.

"The what?"

"Your internal narrator," she said. "The little voice that's always judging, comparing, complaining, and distracting. Notice the dialogue going on inside your head right now, saying that this is good or bad, that this is right or wrong. Take a moment to listen."

The pair fell silent, and Jess felt herself tuning in to the voice that echoed through her mind.

"*This is strange,*" it said. "*There's no voice up here. Oh, wait... Shoot!*"

"Hear it?"

"*She's right!*"

"You're right!" Jess said.

"Every person has that voice, Jess. It's the by-product of every experience each individual has throughout their lives, and its opinions are often what stand in our way of truly connecting with people, of accepting them for who they are, warts and all."

"It's kind of a judgmental jerk," Jess said. She thought about the countless times the voice had whispered in her ear. "I can't exactly get rid of it, can I?"

DAKOTA LAMARRE

Her mind raced, thinking about her relationships with her co-workers and her family.

"I have some warts I need to get past," Jess continued.

"We all do," the woman in the painting answered, glancing back to the man reading his paper.

"How well are you practicing what you preach?" Jess asked.

"Not very well, I'm afraid," the woman said with a sad smile.

"I think I need to apply this with my family right now," Jess said, observing the scene.

"Don't let me hold you back," said the woman in the painting. "I acknowledge you for being so open to this and for transforming from Sally Skeptic to being open-minded. Now, go to your family."

The woman turned her back to the man reading the paper and became just a painting again. As Jess pushed her way through the art gallery doors into the evening air, her inner voice spoke to her.

"*This might work,*" it said.

10

AUTHENTICALLY HUMAN

The discussion with the woman in the painting recharged Jessica's soul.

When she returned home from the gallery that night, Jessica found Paul and Lily at the dinner table. Her initial reaction was to be hurt, maybe even angry, but she focused instead on silencing her inner voice and releasing her perspective. What remained was nothing but curiosity about Paul and Lily's experiences. Instead of wasting time feeling wronged, she asked how their days had gone.

Lily was happy that she had received an excellent grade on one of her assignments. A recent article of Paul's had been a success, opening a door for future projects with a reputable publication. Jessica shared her success with Ravi and recommended that they go out together to celebrate the day. Lily suggested ice cream. Paul and Jessica agreed.

The next morning, despite a train delay and some rain on her walk from the station, she was floating. She felt more connected to her family than she had in months, and she was bursting with excitement for Lily's dance recital that evening.

Nothing was different around the office, but she felt a little more equipped to deal with whatever would come her way. As the afternoon wound down and five o'clock approached, she heard a soft rap at her door. Ravi's head appeared.

"Do you have a minute?" he asked.

"Come on in."

"Whoa," he stopped halfway to her desk. "Nice earrings."

She wasn't sure why she had felt so daring this morning, putting in a pair of artsy, dangly earrings she had picked up in Paris many years ago. It was the first time she had worn them in years, and she had received many compliments.

"Thank you." She gestured for him to take a seat.

"I wanted to build on what we talked about the other day," Ravi said. "I had an idea to expand on our success from re-segmenting the customer data. I think we can replicate the strategy across more of our product lines and see similar results."

Jessica's heart rate increased, anxious that Ravi was coming to her with another idea.

"*That sounds like a lot of extra work, with no guaranteed outcome,*" said the voice in her head. "*It's not worth it.*"

"*Zip it,*" she responded to the voice.

"Tell me more," Jessica said aloud.

Ravi explained how he had studied their customer data and believed they could push more targeted advertising to the right people.

"I like this idea," Jessica said. "Can you put your thoughts into a document and email them to me? I can review them on the train ride home."

"I actually have to leave right now," Ravi replied, nervous but steadfast. "I'm moving in with my girlfriend this weekend, and we want to get a head start. I have to meet her at the truck rental place at five-thirty."

"I didn't know you had a girlfriend," Jessica frowned.

"It never came up," Ravi shrugged. "I'll get something to you over the weekend."

Jessica saw Ravi as more than just a cog in the machine. She admired him for his work ethic and attitude, and his performance and output. Yet, she knew very little about him.

"*You barely know this person,*" Jessica's inner voice said. "*He's more than just your employee. He's a human being.*"

"*I'm working on it,*" she said, stifling her biggest critic.

Jessica wanted to see their working relationship from Ravi's perspective. "Why haven't you brought this idea to me sooner?" she asked. "Wait, let me rephrase that. What prompted you to bring this to me now?"

"You're always busy," Ravi said. "I figured it wasn't my place to put something else on your plate. But I felt like you would be open to hearing it after our lunch yesterday."

Ravi waited for Jessica's reaction, hoping he hadn't misread her openness.

"I'm sorry," she said.

"For what?"

"For not empowering you more in the past and for not fostering an environment where you could share ideas. I'm sorry you haven't been allowed to live up to your full potential. I'm sorry I haven't been coaching you to fight for your ideas even when people like me aren't listening."

Her authenticity and vulnerability dumbfounded Ravi.

"Sometimes, I'm frustrated by your constant ideas," Jessica continued. "It's probably because you remind me of a younger version of myself, and it bothers me that I'm no longer as creative as I can be in my career. I don't want you to end up like this."

She lowered her hands, having raised them to gesture to herself and drive home her point. She waited to see if Ravi would weigh in.

"I'm honored that you're sharing this with me, Jessica," he said. "I admire you and would love to develop in my career to become a lot like you."

As Ravi looked down at his folded hands, Jessica didn't dare move a muscle.

"I see you as incredibly creative and as an amazing role model," he continued. "But I don't want to end up like this deflated version of yourself that you've become since settling into your promotion. Seeing your demeanor change over the past year hasn't gotten me excited for my future here. Lately, I've been wondering if it's better elsewhere. I've been perusing some job boards and have once or twice thought about jumping ship, even though I feel guilty every time I do."

Jessica focused on not taking his words personally or implanting a story where it didn't belong. She waited for Ravi to raise his head.

"Thank you for your honesty," she smiled. "I can see how this job must have been hard on you lately. I'm willing to recommit myself to your learning and development. You're a rock star, and it's my job to help you share that with as many people as possible. Together, we can create an environment where your ideas are used and celebrated, and I think everyone will benefit from the outcomes."

Ravi was baffled by the change in Jessica's demeanor, unsure what it was or how it happened. She realized how strange it must be for him to watch his boss go through such a rapid transformation.

"I have to get going," Jessica said. She wanted to stay and chat but had made a promise to her family. "What comes next? What do you require to put your idea into action?"

"I think I'd like to present it to Maureen, with your help."

"*Well, color me impressed...*" the voice in Jessica's head said.

DAKOTA LAMARRE

Ravi avoided her gaze, nervously awaiting her response.

"I'm more than willing to help you," Jessica said. "And I want to make sure I'm making the most of our time. What else can you do to get ready to present your idea to Maureen?"

Ravi wasn't used to being in control. The managers and directors in the company had fallen into the habit of hijacking their team members' problems and projects as their own. Jessica herself had been a culprit many times.

"I'll get input from other managers on how we can effectively execute the modified campaigns to make sure we're not missing anything," said Ravi. "And I can collect more research on the results of other companies that have used a similar approach."

"Good. That will create a compelling case when we present this to Maureen," Jessica said. "When can you have it done?"

"I'll do it this weekend," he said.

"Are you sure you're going to have enough time? What about the move?"

"Jessica," Ravi replied, pointing to his temple. "I've been marinating this for months; I just never thought it would go anywhere. I only need an hour or two to organize the information and prepare it for a presentation."

After Ravi left, Jessica's mind raced with how she could get the best out of all her team members. She pictured a dozen Ravis. If she could make this vision come to life, their team would be unstoppable.

Gathering her belongings and pulling on her coat, she couldn't wait to get home. Another wonderful evening with her family awaited. Given how much Lily had been practicing for her dance recital, Jessica was sure they would be celebrating again tonight. She checked her watch. She had plenty of time to get home and eat before the recital.

As she turned off her monitor and shouldered her purse, Jessica's door burst open to reveal a tornado.

11

THIS WON'T WORK

Maureen was already in mid-conversation. Jessica froze like a deer caught in headlights.

"... and these reports aren't going to work. I'm going to need you to pull new ones."

Maureen took a seat in front of Jessica's desk, head down as she shuffled through a collection of files.

Maureen noticed the purse on Jessica's shoulder. "Where are you going?"

Jessica couldn't speak.

"I need you to run these again," Maureen continued, holding up a stack of papers. "Gary just told me that he wants to show two years of data for the board to approve our budget."

"But I submitted my team's budget yesterday," Jessica said, eager to escape.

"Now we're apparently doing things differently, Gary decided this morning. This is top priority. I need you to stay and help me fix it. Even though I don't think it's going to work like he thinks it will."

"*Then why are we doing it?*" Jessica asked herself internally. "*Why didn't you tell Gary what you think?*"

Jessica hung up her coat and slowly slid into her chair. She wanted to feel bad for Maureen, sensing her stress, but her frustration at being delayed in getting home to her family devoured any possible sympathy.

It was a recurring joke around the office that Maureen would rather stay late than go home to her empty apartment. If you got in her path, the only thing you could do was hope to get the work done as quickly as possible.

"Anyway," Maureen continued. "We're going to have to figure this out because I promised we would have something to show him by Monday at lunch. He looked so stressed when he came to me, I just wanted to do something that would help him, even if he is really hard to deal with sometimes."

"*I know the feeling,*" said the voice in Jessica's head.

Jessica pulled out her phone to let Paul know that she would be running late and would meet him and Lily at the recital. She couldn't even enter her passcode before Maureen thrust a stack of papers at her.

"Look here," said Maureen, pointing at one of the reports.

Jessica put her phone down as she took the stack from Maureen.

...

It was dark when they took a break, the glowing windows of distant buildings replacing the need for stars.

"I'm going to grab another coffee," Maureen said, rising from her chair. "Do you need anything?"

Jessica ran her fingers through her hair, blinking as she peeled her eyes away from the computer screen.

"No, thanks."

She was trying to be accepting. Maureen was a talented problem solver, a rational thinker, and a hard worker. She had all the qualities of a decent manager. Jessica enjoyed being in the zone with her when they challenged each other and built on each other's ideas.

"*This isn't going to work,*" said Jessica's inner critic as she shuffled through their edited reports. "*You're wasting your time.*"

"Hold on," she replied to it. "*There's an opportunity to learn here. If Gary had involved me in the decision-making process, I could have told him why this new way of reporting won't provide us any more insight than the way we did it before, even though it takes more time to pull the data together.*"

Jessica smacked herself on the forehead with the palm of her hand, realizing that saying these things to herself would never create the change she wanted. If this project didn't work out as planned, she would end up having to clean up the aftermath, which meant it was her responsibility to do something about it. She was playing the role of victim by casting Gary and Maureen as the villains while unconsciously clinging to beliefs like "it's not my job" and "I can't say no to my boss." In reality, she had put herself in this situation by keeping her mouth shut.

Jessica was prepared to voice this when Maureen got back, pleased that at least one piece of learning came from this evening of pointless work. As she glanced at the picture of her, Paul, and Lily in Greece, her determination switched to panic. It was dark outside.

Shuffling through the piled folders on her desk, she found her muted phone, jamming the home button to reveal multiple missed calls and text messages. Her hand reached up, her thumb and forefinger finding her temples in the horrific realization at what she had done. The phone fell from her hand, landing on a stack of papers with a dull thud.

Jessica's eyes were closed, her cheek on the cool surface of her desk when Maureen re-entered the room.

"What's up?" Maureen asked.

It took all Jessica's effort to lift her head.

"I missed my daughter's dance recital."

A shadow of guilt flashed behind Maureen's eyes.

"You should have said something," she took a sip of her coffee.

Jessica shrugged, dead inside.

"*Just another case of mommy letting the family down,*" said the voice inside her head.

"What's left for us to do?" Jessica asked, lifting herself upright.

There was no point in rushing home. The damage was done.

12

FINALLY, THE WEEKEND

The smell of bacon and pancakes wafted through a crack in the bedroom door, accompanied by the happy sounds of a Saturday morning. Paul and Lily were surely dancing around the kitchen while he made breakfast. Jess pulled the covers up over her head as a shriek of Lily's laughter found her ears.

It was nearly midnight when she had arrived home last night, all the lights off except for the one above the front door and the one above the stove. Sneaking into her own home, she chose to forgo the plate of leftovers in the fridge, too defeated to stomach any food.

Anxiety threatened to overcome her again as she commuted home, thwarted only by her sheer exhaustion. Her mind still raced as she snuck into the ensuite bathroom to brush her teeth by the nightlight. Head hitting the pillow, her mind swam with regrets from countless other times when she let her family down.

Having tossed and turned all night, getting little sleep, Jess dreaded facing her husband and daughter this morning.

They had every right to be angry with her. She had been so confident that she would be there, that her days of missing soccer games and dance recitals were coming to an end. Maybe it was the juxtaposition of the successes she had experienced at work to this major failure at home, but she felt splattered, like a bug on a windshield.

The pitter-patter of small feet approached, making her freeze.

"Mommy?" came a tiny voice.

Footsteps shuffled closer, and Lily tugged at the blankets, trying to pull them off her mother. Jess didn't stir, only her hair peeked out above the covers. Waiting, holding her breath, she hated that she was hiding from her child.

After a moment of silence where she felt her daughter's eyes boring into the pile of covers, Jess heard a groan. Lily was leaving.

Why was she so grateful to be left alone?

"It's because you failed them, yet again," said the voice in her head.

"Oh, shut up," she thought back.

Jess rolled over and fell into a restless slumber.

. . .

Standing over her, Paul sighed as he glanced at the alarm clock on Jess's bedside table. She had woken up to him softly whispering in her ear.

"C'mon," he said. "It's time to start your day."

"I can't," she said, pushing the covers down to reveal her tired eyes.

Paul wouldn't take no for an answer. He practically carried her down the stairs, plopping her at the kitchen table and placing a cup of coffee in front of her. Even when Jess was in the wrong, he was still there to support her when she was down.

The clouds lazily parted as Jess took her first few sips of coffee. She finally noticed the first-place ribbon lying just to the left of her placemat. She blinked her stinging eyes at the blue and gold piece of fabric, bringing it closer to her face to examine it more closely.

"She was pretty disappointed last night," Paul said. Jess could feel him watching her. "But she still insisted on putting it at your place so you would see it when you got home."

"I didn't see it last night," Jess said, waves of gratitude for her amazing daughter washing over her. "I just came upstairs and collapsed."

Paul got up from his seat, walking around Jess's chair to embrace her from behind.

"I know you're struggling," he said. "It's okay."

"I don't know how you can forgive me," she answered.

"That's because you haven't forgiven yourself yet," Paul said, though Jess couldn't tell if she imagined a quiver in his voice. Paul's eyes were moist. "Besides, I'm not the one you have to win over."

Jess followed his finger as he pointed over her shoulder to the sliding glass door that led to their backyard. Standing with her hands on her hips and a frown on her face, clearly displeased with her mother, was Lily. When she saw her parents looking at her, she turned on her heel and stormed out of sight. It would have been comical, if Jess wasn't so sad.

Paul leaned down and planted a kiss on Jess's forehead. She felt herself covered in warts.

"Come join us outside when you're ready," he squeezed her shoulder before leaving to join Lily.

Through her commiserating, Jess was struck by the thought that the three stages of a relationship also applied to the relationship she had with herself. Stuck as she was in the warts phase, she wondered how she could get past it and move towards self-acceptance.

"*You are so close-minded with yourself,*" her inner voice said.

"*I have to stop judging my actions as right or wrong and start accepting myself as I am,*" she replied. "*It's in the past. I can't change what's already happened. Look how much fun they're having while I'm sitting here wallowing in self-pity. Be grateful for the abundance of love in your life, and stop taking them for granted. They love you unconditionally; go show them you appreciate it. It's time to change the relationship you have with yourself to be more forgiving and less judgmental."*

She could see Paul chasing Lily around the yard, both of them laughing hysterically.

"*You might be right,*" the voice said.

"*I know I am,*" Jess replied.

Shaking her head, she walked outside to join her family. The first thing she did was pick up her daughter to apologize.

"I'm sorry, darling," she said to Lily. "I wanted so badly to be at your recital, but I got distracted at work. Mommy made a mistake. Can you forgive me?"

Lily considered her mother for a moment, scanning her eyes for sincerity.

"Okay, I forgive you," she said. "I did really good, though. I came in first."

"I know you did. I saw your ribbon. Congratulations," Jess said, putting Lily back down.

Jess was amazed at how quickly Lily had forgiven her and moved on. She could probably learn something from her daughter on this topic.

Sitting on the edge of the staircase from the deck into the yard, she watched her husband and daughter toss a ball back and forth. She allowed herself a flicker of happiness. She was grateful that her family was so supportive and forgiving, even if it still didn't solve her Maureen problem.

Jessica was sure this wasn't the end of their budgeting issue. Monday would roll around, and they would have to manage the situation again, with hardly any new learnings about themselves, each other, or how to solve the problem. What was she going to do about her boss?

"Mom!"

Whack.

Coffee spilled onto her hand as she was jolted from the impact. Lily had mistaken Jess's glossed over glance as an invitation to throw her the ball. Paul laughed first, then Lily. Jess had no choice but to join in, enjoying a therapeutic release of pressure.

As the weight lifted off her shoulders, Jessica remembered an exercise from a college improv class, meant to practice being present. The class started by tossing around one ball, anyone able to throw it to anyone. As it became easy, the instructor would toss another ball into the crowd, and then another. The purpose was to give up your agenda, to sacrifice your attachments, and to be present, acting and reacting in the moment, or you might get hit in the face.

With that, Jess sacrificed the past and the future, realizing it was a simple matter of a shift in belief.

She was back to normal by lunch, asking Lily to recount the previous evening in as much detail as possible, actively listening to her daughter with the utmost joy. Even though a small part of her still felt guilty for missing the recital, she was happy not to have wasted the weekend being miserable.

"Thank you for coming back to us," Paul said, walking up to embrace her from behind as she washed the dishes later. "We miss you."

He was talking about more than just today.

"I miss you both too," Jess said, twisting around to face him, still locked in his arms. "Things are going to get better, I promise. I can't quite explain how I know it yet, but they are."

"I believe you," Paul replied, leaning in for a kiss.

Lying in bed later that night, Jess rolled over to watch her husband sleep. If Paul and Lily could accept her despite her faults, she believed she could do the same with herself. Maybe her warts weren't so unforgivable after all.

Belief Shift: Leaders hold the belief that "I can make a difference" (rather than "it's just the way it is"). This belief shifts their mindset and attitude, inspiring them to act, and act differently. Courage, conviction, and vision help make that possible. Further, leaders don't limit this to themselves, but choose to believe that "employees are people that want to do great work," and they don't really want to be told what to do.

• STAGE 3 •

I AM THE SOLUTION

13

I ACKNOWLEDGE YOU

Jess had stayed present with Paul and Lily for the remainder of the weekend, but something about the train ride into the city today had sent her spiralling into her usual Monday morning feeling of dread.

She had been waiting for her lunch hour, eager to get back to the art gallery. Brushing past the woman in the red dress in *Room in New York*, Jess expected to search through other paintings for some sign of movement.

"Over here," came a soft voice.

Jessica searched up and down the row of paintings until she heard a faint laugh. Her eyes came to rest on a young blonde woman sitting with her mother on a white house's second-story balcony. The young woman in a bathing suit waved to Jess from the painting entitled *Second Story Sunlight*[3].

"So, how'd it go?" the young woman asked.

Jess let out a heavy sigh.

"Oh my," the woman in the painting said, covering her mouth. "That sounds serious."

"Big wins and big losses since we last spoke," Jess nodded.

"Where do you want to start?"

"Biggest win was seeing past Ravi's warts and accepting him exactly as he is. I realized how little I know about his personal life and how much I want to change that. I also unintentionally got vulnerable with him, sharing my perspective and some of my hopes and fears. It flowed naturally from our last conversation, and it created space for him to bring more of his ideas forward."

"Sounds like you've stumbled on the importance of authenticity and vulnerability. What did you experience from the interaction?"

"Possibility," Jess said. "I saw not only better ways for our team to accomplish our goals, but for our team to operate and communicate with one another. Ravi shared an idea that could revolutionize the way our team operates, and he

---

[3] Edward Hopper, *Second Story Sunlight*, 1960, Oil on canvas, 40 3/16 × 50 1/8in. Whitney Museum of American Art, New York, https://whitney.org/collection/works/873, accessed 23 March 2021.

pushed me to be a better leader by requesting my help in presenting it to Maureen himself. It was perfect."

"He was perfect? You were?"

"Everything was," Jess answered. "Warts and all."

"Fantastic," the young woman said, fiddling with her blonde hair. "What else?"

"Well…" Jess struggled to find the best way to continue. "A big loss, that kind of led to a win."

"They often do," the woman in the painting said. "When your head's on straight." They both laughed.

"I missed Lily's dance recital," Jess continued. "Maureen walked into my office at the end of the day on Friday and made me stay late to help her with a project. I ended up missing the recital and beating myself up pretty bad. It took me most of Saturday morning, and the unconditional love of my family, to bounce back."

"Where was the win?"

"I realized that we go through the same three stages of a relationship with ourselves as we do with other people. I tend to create stories about what other people think of me."

"I see," the woman said. "Like with Maureen and your lunch invitation?"

Jess nodded.

"I believed that my family was upset with me," she said. "Even though in reality they were loving and supporting. Thankfully, I figured it out because I would have ruined the entire weekend otherwise. I still don't know what to do about Maureen, though."

DAKOTA LAMARRE

The blonde woman shifted on the balcony railing where she sat, waiting for Jess to quiet her mind.

"What do you want to do?" the woman asked.

Jess frowned as if the question was offensive.

"I want to continue."

The young woman laughed again.

"Just making sure."

Jess glanced down the hall at some of Hopper's other paintings, missing her more mature friends from before.

"*You have warts with a painting?*" said the voice in her head. "*I thought you were done judging people.*"

Jess shook her head, trying to still her inner dialogue, focusing instead on actively listening to what the painting had to say.

"I want to acknowledge you on your journey so far," the young woman said. "The highs and lows, the successes and failures. I've seen you experience some amazing breakthroughs in how you see yourself with your team and your family. You've taken on the work with vigor and excitement, taking action and applying the skills I've shared with you, noticing opportunities to incorporate them into your daily life and reflecting afterward on their impact."

Jess tilted her head, at first in surprise, then in confusion. The woman continued.

"You've shown your ability to shift your beliefs, to build trust with others, and to use your curious mind to accept others exactly as they are. And you've overcome the challenge of your self-resignation and your belief that you're powerless to make a change."

The young woman looked out of the frame at her expectantly. Jess squirmed, wanting her to fill the silence.

"I mean, I guess," Jess finally said. "I was just doing my job. There's still lots of work left to do."

"Stop and think about the impact you're having on the lives of those around you, your team members, and your family, not to mention the changes occurring in your own life. This is a big deal, Jess, and I acknowledge you for it."

Jess allowed herself a breath, the acknowledgment settling over her like a warm blanket. She hadn't realized her thirst for recognition and acknowledgment. It felt like she had gone so long without water, she had forgotten she was thirsty.

"*She's right. You deserve it,*" her inner voice filled the silence.

"Thank you," Jess said aloud. "I appreciate your acknowledgment."

"Thank you for being so coachable."

"What's the next skill?" Jess asked, still uncomfortable with the attention.

"This! You just experienced it!" the young woman said.

Confusion crept back out of hiding. Jess opened and closed her mouth like a goldfish until the young woman smiled at her again.

"I totally missed it," Jess admitted.

"Were you too busy thinking about what was coming next?" the young woman asked in mock frustration. "Fine, I'll say it again."

As she repeated her acknowledgment, Jess listened intently, quieting her mind to experience what was being said.

"Thank you," she said. "That was almost too much."

"Why do you say that?"

"People don't usually go that far in acknowledging others. Usually, a simple 'thank you' is all you get."

"That's exactly why it's important," the young woman said. "Was any of it untrue?"

"It was all accurate," Jess answered.

"That's why you deserve it. None of the things we're discussing here are ordinary, but they're so impactful, it's foolish not to do them. What are you experiencing right now?"

"A little bit of shock," Jess replied. "But mostly warmth."

"What would it mean if everyone on your team could feel like that?"

"It would mean a lot," she said. "Teach me, please."

"Okay," the young woman said, clapping her hands in excitement. "It's straightforward. I call it the A-squared, C-squared principle because the stages build on each other exponentially. First, you acknowledge the *accomplishment*, which might come in the form of a new insight, breakthrough, or result that the person experienced. Then you highlight the *action* that the person took to make that possible."

Jess had taken out her notebook, scribbling notes as the woman continued.

"Then you mention the *characteristics*, or competencies or skill sets, that the person demonstrated throughout their course of action, and then comment on the *challenges* that they overcame to make it possible."

The woman waited for Jess to finish writing.

"That's it! My mother taught me," the woman gestured to the older woman who sat reading on the chair beside her. "And now I get to teach you."

"She must be a wise woman," Jess played along.

"Oh, she is," the young woman said, smiling. "She's constantly encouraging me to better myself and to take a stand for the people I care about. Which reminds me, I have a challenge for you now."

"Not to worry," Jess said, tapping her notebook with her pen. "I'm going to go apply this right now."

"With Maureen?"

Jess hesitated.

"Yes, with Maureen."

"Good," the young woman continued. "But that was only a part of my challenge. Yes, you should acknowledge Maureen, but I would like to see you acknowledge everybody else you see or meet today and throughout the week. Your family, friends, co-workers, the cashier at the coffee shop for getting your order right, everyone."

"That's overkill, isn't it?"

"The homework isn't about the homework, Jess. You can't go to the gym once and emerge in peak physical condition. You can't take one art lesson and become the next Edward

Hopper. It takes practice to master the skills that build your core competencies. If you only acknowledge one or two people, you won't have a chance to develop those muscles. Doing it once or twice won't have an impact on the people around you, either."

Jess pondered the validity of this statement.

"Okay, I'm in," she said.

"How will you know when you're successful?" the young woman asked.

"I could write down every time I acknowledge someone," Jess replied. "Journaling will help me reflect on my growth, and realize how I'm changing into someone who listens, acknowledges, and recognizes, instead of being someone who constantly finds faults."

"I've seen you transform so much in such a short time, and I'm confident you'll also incorporate this new skill into your leadership style."

Jess let the woman's confidence seep into her.

"You're right. I can."

"What are you waiting for?" the woman asked.

Jess turned on her heel and started walking away. She looked back at *Second Story Sunlight* to see the young woman in the painting waving goodbye. She walked with purpose back to the office for a conversation she knew was overdue.

14

PARCHED EARTH

Scrolling through her phone, Jessica checked Maureen's calendar. Nothing came up, which meant she should be in her office.

As she rounded a row of cubicles and the corner office came into view, Jessica could see Maureen seated at her desk, phone to her ear. Jessica knocked out of courtesy but didn't wait to be invited in. She sat down at Maureen's desk and waited for her to hang up the phone.

"What are you…?" Maureen started to ask.

"I need to talk to you," Jessica said before she could finish. "I'm sorry to cut you off, but I need to say some things."

The urgency in Jessica's voice kept Maureen from speaking. Fear flashed in Maureen's eyes.

"I want to acknowledge you, Maureen, for all that you've accomplished in this role. Everyone thought you would be an interim vice-president, and that we would have to fill this position after they found the right person, but you stepped into this role and very quickly proved that you were the right person all along."

Maureen looked at Jessica as if a third ear had sprung out of her forehead.

"Without hesitating," Jessica continued, "you got your hands dirty, taking on new projects, hiring people, staying late, creating and implementing strategic plans, and picking up slack to push our team to keep performing better and better."

The shock on Maureen's face morphed into a grimace, like she was sitting on a sharp object. Still, Jessica went on.

"You've constantly displayed perseverance, tenacity, diligence, attention to detail, and plain hard work. And you've overcome a lack of support and low expectations of your performance. Despite tons of confusion and miscommunication, you've risen to the challenge."

Maureen looked sheepishly acceptant of the acknowledgment, clearly wishing it would end.

"What I'm trying to say, Maureen, is that I'm honored to work with you," Jessica stared deeply into her eyes. "I've let our relationship bring frustration and stress into my life, and that's on me. I'm here to tell you that I'm committed to changing that."

Maureen tried to start a sentence but was unable to find the words. She took a deep breath.

"No one has talked to me like that in a very long time," she finally said.

Jessica kept her lips clamped shut.

"When you first walked in," Maureen continued. "I thought you were going to quit."

"What was that like for you?" Jessica asked.

"I was terrified. I don't know what I would do if you left."

Jessica wondered why she was surprised to hear this.

"I'm not going anywhere," she said.

As she watched Maureen closely, Jessica could see the creases on her boss's forehead stretch and disappear.

"You know, Jessica," Maureen said thoughtfully. "Back home in Jamaica, I grew up in a small farming community. We sometimes had droughts where it didn't rain for a long time. We could see the ocean from the land, but the ground became so hard and compact, the dirt was almost like concrete."

Jessica was amazed that Maureen was sharing a personal story.

"A few clouds could come by, sprinkling the ground with a little rain, but the ground would remain dry and hard. Even with a storm, the water would flow away, and the ground would be dry again by the next afternoon. It would take days of steady rain before the hard earth would soften and accept what it was receiving. I feel like that dry, parched earth right now, and you have brought a little welcome rain into my life.

"I have not had my efforts recognized like that since..." Maureen paused, caught in a memory. "Since my grandmother used to acknowledge me when I was a little girl. She raised me, and making her proud brought me so much peace."

Maureen sighed, visibly relaxing.

"I had forgotten what it felt like," Maureen said.

Her lips stretched into the faintest smile, something that Jessica had rarely seen in their years of working together. She looked angelic. Any tension between the two of them evaporated.

"I know you are up to something," Maureen said, wagging a finger at Jessica. "I don't know what it is, but I like it. Your acknowledgment hasn't fully sunk in yet because I wasn't ready for it, but I'm grateful, and I promise to soften up to accept more of it, and I would like to work at offering you some in return."

"I would like that," Jessica said. "You deserve to be acknowledged, Maureen."

They saw each other more clearly. It was as if a veil that had obstructed their ability to see each other was now gone. In this new realm of communication, they both spoke freely. Jessica asked more about Maureen's childhood; Maureen inquired about Paul and Lily. They quickly covered a lot of ground. The conversation gradually shifted towards work.

"What about you?" Jessica asked. "Do you want Gary's job?"

"What do you think?" Maureen replied. "*He* doesn't even want his job. Why would I want it?"

Both women laughed.

"Do you want mine?" Maureen asked.

Jessica tried to answer but tripped over her words, not wanting to be hurtful but not knowing how to speak the truth.

"That's fair," Maureen said. "I guess I don't make it seem very attractive. To be honest, I sometimes feel threatened by you."

"Where are those feelings coming from?"

"You're such a strong employee," Maureen said. "I thought it would be obvious to everybody that you should be next in line for the vice-president role, and here I am standing in your way."

"My strengths are a complement to yours, Maureen, just like yours are a complement to mine. That's why we're a great team."

They could have continued talking for hours, but they both knew that piles of work still awaited them, demanding their attention for the remainder of the afternoon. Jessica pushed her chair back, almost ready to leave.

"Thank you for being so receptive and open to my acknowledgment," she said to Maureen. "It means a lot to me to be working on our relationship."

"Thank you, Jessica," Maureen replied. "I'm very grateful that you stopped by. This was the best conversation I've had in a long time."

As Jessica pushed her chair back and stood up to leave, she could tell that Maureen meant it.

Jessica was halfway across Maureen's office when a human form of frantic energy burst in, forcing her to duck behind the rapidly swinging door to avoid a collision. It was Gary, and something was wrong.

15

FROM THE TOP

Jessica looked at Maureen. Maureen stared at Gary. The fear in Maureen's eyes was familiar, the same that was in Jessica's eyes when Maureen had entered her office last Friday.

"I thought I said three years of backdated data," Gary said, not noticing Jessica as he made his way towards the desk. He held Jessica and Maureen's report in his hand. "This wasn't what I asked for."

As the shock wore off, Maureen's face settled into a frown. "I'm sure it was two," she said. "I have it written down…"

Maureen flipped through pages of her notebook, hoping to back up her claim.

"It doesn't matter," Gary said, still looking down. "This isn't going to work."

Maureen watched Gary like he was a ticking time bomb. As he sat down and leafed through the papers in his hands, Maureen glanced over his shoulder at Jessica. She quickly looked away as Gary started again. It was clear he had no idea Jessica was in the back corner of the office.

"I thought this new way of budgeting was going to work, but it's not. We're going to have to start from scratch."

He tossed the files onto Maureen's desk, leaning back in his chair and running his hands through his thinning hair. The thought struck Jessica that all the work she and Maureen had done last Friday night, and all that it had cost her, were for nothing.

"What can I do to help?" Maureen asked.

"That's the million-dollar question," Gary replied. "The board is on me about our shrinking revenues and profits. They want better planning, proof that we're going to recover from this year. I feel like I can't count on anyone."

Gary's negativity was polluting the hope that Maureen and Jessica had created together. Jessica still stood in the corner, knowing she had waited too long to now move.

"We can get through this together, Gary," Maureen said in a last attempt to drag him out of his slump.

"How, Maureen? I'm tapped out," he replied. "What am I supposed to do next? I feel like we've tried everything. This environment we're working in, it feels like we can't succeed. I don't know, Maureen. Maybe it's me."

He shifted in his seat, looking uncomfortable.

"Look at this," he poked at his belly bulging out over his belt buckle. "Did I have a gut when you first met me? I used to swim fifty laps a day, and now my doctor has me on cholesterol pills. What's that all about?"

Supported by his elbow on the armrest, he placed his temples between his thumb and forefinger, closing his eyes to take a deep breath. Watching her boss, the little hope that still remained in Maureen's eyes flickered and died. She slumped in her chair, mimicking Gary's posture and breaking Jessica's heart.

"I'm sorry," Gary said after a tense silence. "I'm feeling a lot of pressure right now, and I shouldn't have taken it out on you. I didn't even ask you if you thought this would work before we tried it, and now here we are, as usual. It's my mistake. I just thought this might work..."

He gathered the files he had thrown onto Maureen's desk into a rough stack.

"I'll leave you to it," he said, standing up. "This isn't your problem to deal with. Let's stick with the process we had before. I'll find a way to deal with the board."

Maureen opened her mouth to say something but couldn't find the right words. As Gary turned to exit, he saw Jessica standing in the corner. His face flushed, her presence making his display of vulnerability and doubt even more embarrassing. He looked frustrated, sad, and pathetic all at once, and more than anything Jessica wanted to give him a hug.

"I, uh… hi," he cleared his throat, then left the office with his head down.

The silence was palpable. Jessica stood ten feet away from Maureen, but it felt like they were on different planets. She walked towards the desk and sat down in the same chair Gary had occupied. It was still warm.

Maureen avoided eye contact, so Jessica waited in silence.

"I don't know why I feel so weak right now," Maureen finally said. "I'm sorry you had to see that. It was wrong for you to be here for our drama."

"It's not right or wrong," Jessica said. "It just is."

The voice in Jessica's head was trying to make itself heard, to draw her out of the present, but the only thing that mattered to her right now was Maureen. They sat in silence, Maureen processing the ups and downs of everything that had transpired.

"Do you not sit with her in her sorrow and love her unconditionally?" Jessica heard the voice of her painted friend.

"I'm here with you," Jessica said. Maureen slowly nodded.

Jessica didn't know how long they sat like this. Seasons could have changed outside the window, or seconds could have ticked by on the clock. It didn't matter. Finally, Maureen lifted her gaze and spoke.

"Thank you," she said. "I'm fine."

Jessica inclined her head, checking if it was true.

"Really, I am," Maureen said. "Thank you for staying here with me."

"It was my privilege," Jessica replied.

She stood up again, keeping her eyes on Maureen.

"I want to take you for lunch tomorrow," Jessica said. "My treat."

Maureen looked like she wanted an excuse to get out of it, but Jessica wouldn't let her make one.

"I would like that," Maureen finally replied.

As Jessica rode the elevator to the lobby that evening, she reflected on the afternoon. She saw an opportunity to change the way she and her boss worked together. It was time for her to share her image of a brighter future with Maureen. It was time for Jessica to enroll her boss in her vision.

16

CONFRONTATION

Up and down the hall, Jess scanned Hopper's paintings.

"There's an easier way to do this," she said to the empty room.

Dust motes spiraled through rays of sunlight as she searched for her friend. She came to a painting of a woman in a red dress standing on a stoop with her arms crossed, a large-brimmed hat shielding most of her face from sunlight. Jess eyed the painting, called *South Carolina Morning*[4], with suspicion until it finally moved.

---

[4] Edward Hopper, *South Carolina Morning*, 1955, Oil on canvas, 30 3/8 × 40 1/4in. Whitney Museum of American Art, New York, https://whitney.org/collection/works/789, accessed 23 March 2021.

"Back so soon?" the woman in the painting said, uncrossing her arms and leaning against the door frame.

"This really is a roller coaster," Jess replied.

"Tell me."

"It went great with Maureen," Jess said. "It took her a while to accept my acknowledgment, but once she did, it opened up a whole new world of communication for us."

She hesitated, not knowing how to continue.

"And then Gary threw a wrench into everything."

"How so?" the woman asked.

"He came in and complained to her about his own mistake and damaged the progress Maureen and I made."

"Were you hoping that things would get easier?"

Jess thought carefully about her response.

"I know I can't control the actions of others, but I hoped that the people in power wouldn't be such an obstacle to creating change."

"Are you equipped to handle these obstacles?" asked the woman in red.

"With my team under me, yes. But how can I possibly drive change in the executive offices? I know how hard Gary has it, and I truly believe that he wants to improve things for us, but what am I supposed to do? It's not like I can barge into his office and demand he become a better leader. I can't create real change. It has to come from the top."

Jess's blood pressure rose, a hint of anxiety invading the corners of her mind as she lamented how impossible it was to change the way her company's executives operated.

"Why don't you tell me a bit more about acknowledging Maureen," the woman said.

"It was the same as when you acknowledged me," Jess answered. "At first, she was surprised, then awkward and uncomfortable, and then grudgingly acceptant while trying to make it end as soon as possible. When she finally opened up to me, it was amazing. I got to know her better in the ensuing fifteen minutes than I have throughout our entire working relationship."

"And what's new in that relationship for you?" the woman asked.

"The possibility of having a great relationship with my boss."

Jess wondered why she wasn't more excited. She had wanted this for ages. Why wasn't she doing cartwheels up and down the hallway?

"What's still there for you?" the woman asked.

"It's not likely that things will continue to improve unless we get Gary to shift his beliefs too. Why can't Maureen do with Gary what I'm doing with her?"

"Why can't she?" the woman challenged.

Jess was at a loss for words.

"Why are you so confrontational today?" Jess asked.

The woman in the painting crossed her arms again, a stern expression on her face.

"Sometimes it's important for us to say things to each other that we would rather avoid saying," the woman responded. "Sometimes we have to acknowledge our fears and confront each other's problem beliefs and behaviors."

Jess was taken aback by her friend's abruptness.

"You've come in here complaining about others before, acting like you're not in a position to drive change, and you're doing it again," the woman in the painting said. "The impact is that you're robbing yourself of all your power to create change, and your negativity is one hundred percent effective. I'm left feeling frustrated because I want to help you realize that the people surrounding you can help you through the remainder of this journey."

Jess's defenses rose, even though the woman in the painting wasn't critical or emotional. This reaction confused her because no part of the woman's observation blamed or framed Jess as wrong. She was just objectively stating facts.

"*Who does she think she is?*" said Jess's inner voice, right on cue. "*Sure, it's easy to talk about creating change from inside a painting. I bet she wouldn't be so critical if she were out here working with me.*"

"That's not fair," Jess responded. "I think I've put a lot of work into this, taken a lot of action, and have seen some pretty remarkable results so far. I don't think it's right for you to say that I'm not doing enough."

"That's not what I said," the woman replied. "I said that your complaining about others is sapping all of your power away from you, and it's frustrating to watch you go through this."

"What do you want me to do? I've already worked on my relationships with my team members and with my boss. Now you want me to go after her boss too? I can't change how Gary chooses to run the company."

The woman smiled and said, "I'll let you think about that for a moment."

"I'm missing the lesson again, aren't I?" Jess asked. "I'm too busy trying to make myself right."

"I'll repeat myself," the woman said. "Your complaining about being powerless is making you powerless, and it's frustrating watching your self-sabotage. You're trying to convince yourself that this is impossible, and you're turning it into a self-fulfilling prophecy. You're making it come true."

Jess tried not to rush to respond, to silence the need to prove herself right and get to the essence of what the woman was trying to communicate.

"Maybe I need to figure out how I could stop doing that," Jess said.

She held up a finger to let the woman know she had more to say. She was getting thoughtful about the situation, her open-mindedness returning.

"I want to stop complaining," Jess continued. "And I need to see results. What if I taught the skills to others so they could share them with the people around them? If I can't get facetime with Gary to spread these skills to him myself, what if I empowered someone who could? Like Maureen?"

Jess gasped as she heard her own words.

"Do you see what just happened?" the woman asked, her face brightening.

Jess liked the destination but wasn't entirely clear on how she had arrived there. The woman in the painting explained.

"You created your own solution because I confronted you, without judgment, blame, or guilt, and because I didn't react to your defensiveness, take on your problem as my own, or let you change the subject."

It took a moment to sink in, but on reflection, it made perfect sense.

"Okay, teach me the formula," Jess said, pulling out her notebook to write it down.

"Step one is to state what happened, without blame, guilt, or emotion. To confront easily, you must provide a concrete example that is concise and judgment-free. Next, you share the impact of that action, again, free from judgment. Third, you describe how it made you feel, without making your feelings their fault. And the fourth and critical step is, you shut up. If they're not ready to create their own solution, you repeat the process until they are."

Jess paused her note-taking.

"You shut up?" she asked.

"Don't allow yourself to get dragged down the rabbit hole," the woman said. "The other person is likely to get defensive, trying to shift the blame or justify their actions, like you just did. Remember, you're in control of how you react to their reaction. You absolutely must remain open-minded and objective until they're willing to do the same, as I just demonstrated."

"I'm going to apply this skill with Maureen at lunch tomorrow," Jess said.

"You're confident that you'll be able to confront her easily and effectively?"

Jess slid her notebook back into her purse.

"It's simple enough, though I know it may not be easy."

"And what will be the impact?"

"I'll prove to myself that real change can come from anywhere, which I'm sure will boost my confidence enough to bring this to the rest of the team," Jess said. "I think we might just stand a chance."

"You *think*?" the woman asked.

"I know," Jess chuckled.

As she thought about how far she had come, Jess was suddenly sad.

"What is it?" the woman asked.

"We're almost done here, aren't we?"

The woman in the painting leaned against the doorway again, pushing up the brim of her hat, her expression softening.

"Almost."

Jess stared down at her feet.

"What are you experiencing?" the woman asked.

"Sadness," Jess answered. "I'm going to miss you."

"I'll never truly leave you, Jess," the woman said. "As long as you're committed to this journey, I'll always be by your side."

"This isn't it, though, is it?"

"I think one more meeting will suffice," the woman said. "There's still one more skill for you to learn."

Jess smiled broadly. She was ready to go home and see her family, and to meet with Maureen.

"This has been the learning phase for you," the woman said. "Now it's time for action. Get excited because this is the opportunity you've been waiting for."

From this new perspective, Jessica's sadness wasn't so raw.

"I like the way you think," she said to the Hopper painting.

"I learned everything I know from wise people like you," the woman responded. "You are the solution, Jess."

The woman in the painting pushed off the wall, crossing her arms and returning to her original position. Jess mimicked the woman's posture, crossing her arms and looking at the painting while she processed the latest information. She slowly turned and walked away, her mind racing.

She left the gallery smiling. She knew it was time to be released back into the wild to practice and master these skills.

17

ENROLLING

The air smelled of flowers.

"I can't believe I've never been here before," Maureen said.

Jessica had taken her to the sculpture garden adjacent to the art gallery for their planned lunch. The water fountain's gentle burbling combined with the sunshine to warm their surroundings and their souls.

"A slice of paradise in the concrete jungle," Jessica smiled as she took in the familiar surroundings. "This is where Paul and I came on our first date. Some of my favorite artworks are inside."

Gazing up at the massive building's stained glass windows, a pang of sadness hit her and then washed away. This sadness had been coming in waves since she had left the gallery the previous evening, lapping at the shores of her emotions.

"I love your outfit," Maureen said, gesturing to Jessica's clothes as they found a seat and unpacked their take-out Greek food.

Jessica had kicked her attire up another notch. She wore a deep blue blouse, a black skirt with white dots, short heels with sapphire gemstones, accessorizing with an extra ring on her finger and matching earrings.

"Thank you," Jessica said. "I used to dress like this all the time. I promised myself I would more often."

The pair engaged in small talk until Jessica couldn't hold back any longer.

"About what happened with Gary yesterday..." she said.

"He's under a lot of stress," Maureen shrugged. "But I knew his new way of doing budgets wasn't going to work."

"And you didn't speak up about it..."

"What's the point?" Maureen asked through a mouthful of souvlaki. "He's the president of the company. I work for him."

The trickling of the water fountain filled the silence between them.

"I have to tell you something that I'd rather not tell you," Jessica said.

Maureen put down her wrap and wiped her hands, looking like she was getting ready for something painful.

"Gary comes to you when he feels like his plans are failing and tells you we're going to try something new or that you're not doing enough. You take on more work, which you then kill yourself to complete or delegate to us. It happened yesterday, and it's happened in the past."

Maureen was caving in on herself, waiting for this to be over.

"You end up working insane hours and expect all of us to do the same. What's asked of you and us often doesn't align with the company's goals, and we end up frustrated and overworked, wondering if it's going to make a difference."

Maureen sat in silence.

"I feel like a puppet and that I have no say in this organization. I feel like my hard work isn't appreciated, or even asked for, but thanklessly demanded. I also feel like I'm not using my creativity to its full capacity, which tells me that opportunities are slipping through the cracks. And I would hazard a guess that you feel the same way."

Jessica watched as Maureen took a drink, her hand shaking as she put the cap back on her water bottle.

"Are you saying that I don't know how to run my team?" Maureen asked. "Because that's not what you were saying yesterday. Yesterday, you acknowledged the pressure that I'm under and that I was never expected to succeed in this role. Now you're saying that I'm a bad boss?"

Maureen was ready to fight, to defend herself. Jessica could only imagine what the voices in her head were saying to her right now. Jessica was determined to stand firm, knowing that she could make her boss better by doing so.

"I did not say that," Jessica answered. "I said that when Gary dumps work on you, and it trickles down to us, our team ends up overworking, often without getting any closer to our goals. The result is that I, and others on our team, feel like our talents are ignored."

"That's just the way it is," Maureen responded. "Gary's the top dog, Jessica. I can't exactly tell him no. What do you expect me to do?"

Jessica repeated herself, and Maureen defended herself. The cycle continued for what seemed like an eternity. Whenever her patience wavered, she thought of the Hopper paintings inside the gallery. Finally, after Jessica had repeated herself yet again, Maureen changed her response.

"I guess we should talk about how I behave with Gary so that we can get out of this vicious cycle."

Jessica perked up like a dog when their owner's car pulls into the driveway, and yet, Maureen seemed deflated.

"What are you experiencing right now?" Jessica asked.

"I don't see how it's even possible to change how I interact with Gary," Maureen sighed.

"Do you feel like he wants help? That he wants to be better?"

"Yes."

"Would you do anything in your power to help him if you could?" Jessica asked.

"Of course," Maureen replied. "But it would take a miracle…"

"That's how I used to feel about you," Jessica said.

Maureen frowned as she turned towards Jessica.

"Maureen, what's happened to our relationship over the past few days?"

Maureen paused, reflecting on the open communication that she was experiencing with Jessica.

"It can happen that quickly," Jessica continued. "I don't think either of us could have predicted even a week ago that we would be enjoying lunch together today. And yet, here we are. All because I started thinking and acting differently."

"What *have* you been up to?" Maureen asked.

"You wouldn't believe me if I told you," Jessica chuckled.

Maureen cocked her head, curious about Jessica's inside joke, but still focused on her proposition.

"Picture this," Jessica continued. "A bullpen where people aren't afraid to laugh, where people are happy to see us, excited to talk with us about their work, their challenges, and their wins. Everyone feels powerful and motivated, and they want to come into the office in the morning. We're doing our best work, sharing our best ideas, and delivering better results. We're all doing less, accomplishing more, and making a difference for the company, ourselves, and each other."

"I don't know how you're planning to pull this off, but I guess I trust you," Maureen said after the pair had returned from their shared daydream. "I'm sold."

"I wasn't selling, Maureen," Jessica smiled. "I was enrolling."

It was as if Jessica stood on one side of a threshold, holding her hand out for Maureen to join. Hesitant, unsure of where the journey would take her, Maureen had reached out and clasped Jessica's hand. She had taken the first step.

DAKOTA LAMARRE

Jessica shared some of her new skills. Maureen gradually warmed up to the world of possibility that Jessica was proposing. They role-played possible conversations between Maureen and Gary and others on their team.

As they created together, Jessica could see a bright future forming in Maureen's eyes. There was a possibility there that hadn't existed an hour ago, a shimmer of hope flickering like a candle in a dark room. Jessica found that when Maureen wasn't thinking about how impossible change was, she had a talent for brainstorming ways to improve their team culture. Maureen outlined ideas that had lain dormant since becoming interim vice-president. Jessica wondered what other treasures awaited in the minds of her team members.

It was almost amusing watching Maureen's defenses rise and fall, seemingly at random. She would dive into an idea, declare it impossible, then do a complete one-eighty again to convince herself that she could make it so. Jessica observed and listened, mostly silently, occasionally adding a comment, and acknowledging Maureen regularly. Wiping a spot of tzatziki from the corner of her mouth, she didn't hide her satisfied smile, happy that her boss was also becoming her disciple and maybe even her friend.

They had much more to discuss, but the lunch hour was over. Jessica couldn't remember when they had worked so well together. Their ideas built upon themselves as they planned for the future. She also couldn't remember when she had seen Maureen smile so much.

As they walked back towards the office, past the art gallery, Maureen touched Jessica's arm to stop her.

"Could you take me one day?" she asked, pointing towards the entrance.

"Of course," Jessica replied. "Just, not today."

"*I still have some unfinished business in there*," her inner voice said.

"Of course," Maureen said, then continued on her excited rant about how she had always wanted to focus on reshaping their team's meeting rhythm.

Jessica was only half-listening to Maureen as they walked back to the office. She was thinking about the impact Maureen and Ravi would have on the people in their lives. Jessica had equipped them with simple and practical skills and the confidence to apply them. She envisioned not only the happy faces of Maureen, Gary, Ravi, Paul, and Lily, but also the faces of hundreds of their friends and colleagues.

Not only was her vision coming to life, it was evolving into something much bigger. It was creating possibilities more meaningful and noble than she ever imagined.

Belief Shift: Most managers have bought into the belief that real change can only be initiated from the top and must cascade down. This leads to disempowerment ("hey, it's not my job"). Leaders know that change and culture shift can start and spread from any point on the organizational chart and then go viral. You can leverage the skills shared throughout this book so that others around you also become people that initiate and spread a culture shift.

DAKOTA LAMARRE

• STAGE 4 •

I WIN ONLY WHEN WE ALL WIN

18

PILLOW TALK

It was time to come clean.

Jess's hands cupped a mug of hot tea, her legs tucked under her as she gazed at Paul across the couch. With the carpool taking care of Lily's rides to and from soccer practice, and Jess home from work at a reasonable hour, it was almost strange to have the house to themselves.

"You're going to think I'm crazy," she said.

"I already think you're crazy," Paul laughed. "What is it?"

Jess started recounting her story from the past few weeks, of the building pressure and the breaking point in the stairwell, of being guided to the art gallery by some unseen, ethereal voice.

"Where we had our first date?" he asked.

She nodded and continued.

"And then, you'll never believe it. The paintings started talking to me."

He nearly spit out his drink.

"Sorry, what?"

"I know, it sounds ridiculous. Maybe it is," Jess said. "But, throughout the past few weeks, various characters from Edward Hopper's paintings have been coaching me to become a better leader. I wanted to share my story with you."

"Okay," he said, putting his drink down and shifting to face her. "I'm not sure what to do with that information. I've noticed your demeanor changing lately, but now I'm wondering if I should be worried about you."

"It's not like that," she said.

He stared at her incredulously, not quite believing what she said, probably worried that she was suffering some sort of psychotic break.

"Are you okay?" he asked.

Jess laughed.

"Yes, Paul, don't worry," she replied. "This is a happy story."

"So, this is real?" he said, skeptical.

"Whether it's real or not doesn't matter," Jess replied. "Let me get to the important part."

"Okay," he said. "Sorry. Go on..."

He fell silent, though he still eyed her with suspicion.

"I've been applying the principles I've learned and have already seen amazing results," she continued. "I've connected with Maureen and Ravi more in the past few weeks than in my entire time working with them."

"What's different?" Paul asked.

"I used to feel like I couldn't say no, like I didn't have a choice," Jess said. "I was like a piece of driftwood stuck in the flow of a rushing river. Now, I feel like I'm still on the river, but I'm in a boat with a rudder and an engine. I can steer, speed up, and slow down, and even head to shore if I want to."

Paul nodded.

"And what's happening because of that?"

He seemed to have moved past his concern for her sanity, now playing the role of curious interviewer.

"Ravi is volunteering for projects. We're communicating openly and enjoying each other's company. He's sharing his best ideas, making sure they aren't pushed aside or hijacked, and solving his own problems."

"That's huge! What comes next?"

"I have Maureen enrolled. We need to formalize how we're going to move forward together. I want to bring this to the rest of my team, and hopefully the entire company."

Paul slowly nodded, thoughtfully processing what Jess was saying.

"I promise that things will get a whole lot better," she continued. "I will work fewer hours and get more accomplished. I want to come home on time, excited and empowered, instead of drained and deflated. I realize now that I make the rules, and I'm going to see this culture shift through to the end."

"What's changed?" he asked. "From before to now?"

"Me hitting rock bottom. I think that's what it took to be open-minded enough to shift my beliefs, to notice the opportunity to build something better. Now I want to make sure other people don't have to sink as low as I did before realizing that change can come from anywhere. I want to help them understand that they can create change wherever they want, as long as they're first willing to transform themselves from within."

They talked and laughed, basking in the rays of their bright future. Jess explained more and more about the skills and the opportunities they created with her teammates.

"You're writing this down, right?" Paul asked.

"You think I should?"

"Jess, I think you have to," he said. "Writing it down makes it real and concrete. You also allow others to look at the content objectively and to make edits to strengthen it or adapt it to their conditions. Plus, there's the whole angle of conversations with paintings. Who knows, maybe you write this down, and it ends up helping millions."

She hadn't thought of writing down these skills and belief shifts and documenting her journey. Now that Paul mentioned it, it seemed irresponsible not to.

"If this stuff works as well as you claim, and I believe you wholeheartedly that it will, then it shouldn't be too hard to find an hour or two each week to work on this project together," Paul said. "I think this could be a great opportunity for you to leave your creative mark on the business world."

"I love you," Jess blurted. Paul beamed. "Thank you for supporting me and for being such a good father to Lily. I know it hasn't been easy lately. I haven't been the best partner or co-parent. I really appreciate you."

Paul bowed his head in acceptance of her acknowledgment. When he looked up, he had an extra twinkle in his eye.

"While we're on the topic of celebrating," he said, referencing the skill Jess had shared earlier. "Lily won't be home for at least another hour…"

"I can't imagine what you're getting at," she teased.

19

FAREWELL FOR NOW

Jess didn't have to search the paintings.

She stood with her hands on her hips in front of a painting named *Automat*[5], which featured a lonesome woman sipping a coffee. Her right hand was bare and holding the mug, and her left hand was gloved.

"I'm ready," Jess said.

---

[5] Edward Hopper, *Automat*, 1927, Oil on canvas, 28 1/8 × 35 in. Des Moines Art Center, Des Moines, https://emuseum.desmoinesartcenter.org/objects/41752/automat, accessed 23 March 2021.

The woman in the painting brought the mug to her lips, took a slow sip, then placed it back down on the saucer with a clink.

"You were sad when we last spoke," she said. "What are you experiencing now?"

"Excitement," Jess responded, thinking of last night with Paul. "I'm excited to continue developing these skills in myself. More than that, I'm excited to enroll others in this journey, helping them shift their beliefs, teaching them the skills, coaching them to apply them, then supporting them to do the same with others, making this movement go viral. I can't wait to see what happens next once this new way of interacting gains traction beyond my colleagues and family. I think we've created something with the potential to help a lot of people."

"You sound like a very different person from a few weeks ago," the woman said, fingering the coffee cup's handle. "What changes are you noticing in yourself?"

Jess recalled her recent dramatic transformation. She once believed it wasn't her place to take action, but now she knew that change was well within her grasp. She thought of her initial resistance, then building her confidence, and the results she had already seen. She was ready to see her mission through to completion.

"I believe now that I don't have to accept things the way they are. I'm done being a victim, and I'm done with other people making themselves victims too."

"That sounds very powerful," the woman said.

"I've learned that assigning blame doesn't help," Jess continued. "There are no villains here, and by seeking out people to blame, I've made myself the victim. Instead of laying blame, which makes people fear being wrong and afraid to take action, I can inspire the accountability required to make the most of every situation, both the failures and the successes."

Excitement coursed through Jess's body. Not the nervous excitement that comes from fear, but the calm, level-headed intensity that accompanies someone living their purpose. Jess pulled a folder from her bag, opening it to scan the first page.

"What do you have there?" the woman asked.

"Paul recommended that I write all this down so that I can share with others," Jess said.

"What do you think about his suggestion?"

"Writing it down inspires me and keeps me accountable, and it helps me track how it evolves. Plus, it helps me get my team involved."

The woman lifted her gloved hand to adjust the brim of her yellowed hat.

"All these commitments, how will you make this transformational culture shift possible?" she asked.

As Jess pondered how she would execute her goals, her eyes wandered to the window and the sculpture garden outside.

"First, by using these skills in my own life consistently until they've become like muscle memory. Second, by explaining what I'm doing, helping people shift their beliefs, enrolling and teaching them to use the skills in their own lives. And third, by empowering and supporting them to make it go viral by coaching them through sharing the skills with others."

"And how will you measure your success along the way? How will you know when you're fulfilling what you've set out to accomplish?"

This is the question that Jess had been avoiding asking herself since the previous night.

"I'm struggling with this," she admitted. "I know that my success is reflected in the success of those around me. I'll know I'm successful when I see the impacts in the lives of people to whom I haven't directly taught the skills. Those tertiary impacts will mean that this has grown much bigger than me, that the people I've coached are now coaching other people through belief shifts and sharing the skills to be empowered to do the same with even more people."

"Those are the requirements of the contract you're making with yourself. How will you measure your success along the way?"

"I'm struggling to come up with a system to measure those impacts," Jess said. "What would that even look like?"

"I don't know, Jess. What would that look like?"

Jess thought and thought, the answer slipping through her fingers like smoke.

"This is the last skill, isn't it?"

The woman in the painting inclined her head as Jess continued to search for the answers.

"It is," Jess said. "I know it is."

"This is the skill of contracting," the woman said. "I call it the RCM principle. First, you must define the *requirements* of the contract, what each party needs from the other. Next, you must list the 'how we will work together' of the *contract*. These are the ways in which you intend to work together to make the requirements possible. Finally, you must add some *metrics*, some methods of measuring performance along the way."

"I'm hung up on how to establish metrics to goal attainment when it's not a clear business outcome," Jess said. "How can I measure qualitative results?"

"If you could attach success metrics to accomplishing your goals, what would you be measuring?"

Seconds stretched into minutes, grains of sand slowly trickling through the hourglass as their stare-off continued. Finally, the answer poured out of her.

"I have a handful of skills to incorporate into my life," Jess started. "There's obviously a measurement of the number of times I apply them in a given week. I think there's also an opportunity to measure how well I use each skill."

Jess looked up at the painting.

"Can I use a self-rating scale on something like how well I use the skills each week? That seems so arbitrary."

"What do you think?" the woman asked.

"I'll do it," Jess answered. "The numbers could be combined to give me an overall score for each skill, each week, which would allow me to track my progress over time."

"Aren't you forgetting something?" the woman in the painting looked at her expectantly.

Jess cocked her head, like a curious dog.

"The others!" she said, realizing her oversight. "This only works when I'm spreading these skills to others. When we hit critical mass, that's when we'll have created a transformational culture shift."

"So, how do you effectively measure the culture shift?"

"I need to get others to realize what I'm doing, to be open to a belief shift, learning these skills themselves, and applying them with the people on their teams. I need to measure, not just the number of times I use the skills, but the number of times I've taught the skills to others, and the number of times they've taught the skills to even more people."

Jess flipped open her notebook, and using a pen from her purse, began scribbling lines and tables. When she had finished, a rough sketch of a scoring matrix stared up at her.

"What's new for you, right now?" the woman asked, watching with pride as Jess marked up her notebook. Jess had almost forgotten where she was, lost in the passion of her work.

"I feel creative again," she replied, coming back to the conversation. "More creative than I've felt in years."

"Is this something concrete you could use to help these beliefs and skills go viral throughout your company?"

Jess nodded vigorously, her earrings jangling with the movement.

"What comes next?" the woman asked.

GEORGE ANASTASOPOULOS

"I share it with everyone on my team, enrolling each of them, and seeing what they can add."

"Good," the woman said. "What else is there for us to discuss?"

The moment had come, the one Jess had been both anticipating and dreading.

"I'm ready," she said. "I don't feel stressed or pressured to do any of this. I don't feel trapped anymore. I feel alive and inspired! And I finally feel like I'm not alone."

The woman in the painting smiled with sad eyes at Jess's last words.

"You don't have to be alone if you don't want to be," Jess said to her painted friend. She wished she could take the painting home with her.

"You are ready," agreed the woman in the painting. "You have the skills to take this vision out of your imagination and bring it fully into the real world."

"So this was just in my imagination?" Jess asked.

"Maybe it was, maybe it wasn't," the woman in the painting responded. "Does not knowing make it any more or less real?"

"No," Jess said. "No, it doesn't matter either way. Thank you."

"It was my pleasure," the woman responded. "Thank you, Jess, for choosing to be open-minded, for being coachable, for not clinging to old beliefs, for creating new habits, and for refusing to give up. You'll continue to experience setbacks and speed bumps, but now you're equipped to handle them."

Jess was nodding so much, she resembled a bobble-head on the dashboard of a car.

"Whenever you're overwhelmed, remember that I'm always with you, and there are always others out there to help. And if you're ever in a pinch, you can visit me here."

The woman gestured, one hand still gloved, the other bare, to the edges of her frame and the gallery beyond.

"Goodbye, Jess," she said. And with that, Jess's painted friend froze.

"Goodbye," Jess said, her heart full of gratitude and excitement.

20

REQUIREMENTS

Ravi's foot-tapping reached a crescendo. Jessica looked up at him over the top of the document.

"Sorry," he said. "I'm nervous."

"Don't be," she flipped the page. "It's awesome."

Ravi had leveraged the data from their recent successful campaign. He outlined how they could re-segment their customer data to run all their campaigns more effectively and cheaper at scale. She made an incision to his plan with her red pen.

"This is pretty much ready," Jessica said. "I acknowledge the initiative you've taken and the persistence you've shown in bringing this idea into reality. Before I share my feedback,

I'm wondering what you think you can do to continue developing this project."

"It needs some polishing, and I think we should dig a little deeper into this data here." Twisting his hand so Jessica could see his copy of the report, Ravi tapped at one of the data sets with the butt of his pen. "And I can get input from the other managers before bringing the final edits to you."

"Sounds like a plan," Jessica said. "When will you have these changes completed?"

"By the end of today."

She handed the report back to him.

"Then I'll set something up with Maureen on Thursday or Friday," she said. "You and I will go over final edits on Wednesday, and we'll practice your pitch. Are you feeling ready to present this to Maureen?"

Ravi's eyes widened, his excitement evident.

"I'm not quite ready," he said. "But I'm confident."

It was a welcome change to be building up her team members so they could speak for themselves. Jessica was ecstatic at the prospect of watching Ravi's career continue to progress now that he was helping craft a culture and a team that would support him.

"Speaking of getting ready," Jessica said. "I have something I want to share with you."

Jessica pulled a folder out of her desk, opening it to the front page of the document.

"Before I get your input on this, I'd like to talk about how we're going to proceed in our working relationship. I'm sure you've noticed how much attention I've been putting towards our team culture, and I want to get you involved. Are you ready to be a leader in creating an environment where all of us are sharing our best ideas, celebrating each other, working fewer hours, and getting more meaningful work accomplished?"

Ravi nodded, Jessica's vision reflected in his eyes.

"First, I want to know what you require of me as a manager," she said.

"What I require of you?" he asked.

"What do you need from me to do your job the best you can?" Jessica elaborated.

Ravi scratched his chin, pondering his response.

"I need you to listen," he said. "And to be open to my ideas."

Jessica made sure not to interrupt him and to calm the voice inside her head. She took notes, showing that she was listening and fully intended to take action.

"I need you to be straight with me when you think I can be doing better and to keep me pushing for my ideas. And I'd like you to help me develop myself as a leader and help me create ways we can better engage our team."

"That's a lot to unpack," Jessica said. "Like what 'better' means to you, and what behaviors of yours I can look for to know when you're giving up. I'd like to explore how you define a leader, and develop ways to help engage the team. This is more than we can get into right now, but I hope you can see that I'm writing this down, and I promise we'll focus on each one of these points very soon. For right now,

I acknowledge your courage in being candid and telling me what you need."

She handed over the document.

"This is one of the ways we're going to achieve the outcomes you've shared. This is what I require of you, to make sure that everyone on our team—everyone in the entire company—doesn't have to ask for the things you just asked for."

"I see it now. This isn't a normal project plan," said Ravi. "You've changed some of your beliefs about managing and leading. I see the distinctions you've captured here, and they make so much sense. It feels good when you treat me like a human being and not just an employee," Ravi said. He pointed to the document as he looked up at Jessica. "Is it working?"

"What are you noticing that's different around here?"

Ravi tapped his foot again as he scanned his memory banks for examples from the past weeks, his lips stretching into a smile.

"You've been more relaxed, and I've seen Maureen smiling a few times in the last few days, which is new for her. It feels like we're doing less but accomplishing more." He gestured to his report resting on his lap. "And this, having the opportunity to bring my ideas to life, well, it'll make a difference."

Ravi scanned Jessica's document again, picturing the benefits this could bring to the team.

"Big project…" he said. "Although, I guess it's less of a project and more of a way of being."

"A journey, not a destination," Jessica smiled. "Is it worth it?"

"I can't think of anything more worthwhile," he replied, their minds and spirits aligned.

"I see here, in the section on contracting," Ravi pointed to the document, "it says we need metrics for measuring performance. What are you proposing?"

"I was hoping you could help with that," she said.

"Why don't we ask the team?" he said instantly. "We could introduce feedback surveys, and monthly meetings to celebrate and acknowledge our accomplishments, both individually and as a group. And some non-business-related metrics, like the number of times we hear people laughing, or the number of times we all leave on time each week. But it's their success, so we should ask them."

Jessica sat back and watched his mind at work. Ravi had already scribbled multiple lines of notes in his notebook before speaking again.

"What comes next?" he asked.

"You and I will meet weekly for the next few weeks to develop these skills in you. If you'll notice, the goal isn't just to shift our own beliefs and develop these skills in ourselves, but to teach others and enroll them. Then, coach and support those people to do the same, making it go viral and transforming the company. I'm hoping you'll be one of the first of these 'evangelists.'"

Ravi was taken aback by the responsibility and trust her request assumed.

"What's your reaction to my offer?" Jessica asked.

"If you had asked me a few weeks ago," Ravi said. "I probably would have told you I can't handle it. But now, I know I can."

"What's different?"

"You," he said. "And us. It's in the air. Things are just better."

"I suppose they are," she said.

"And, what about going upwards with this?" Ravi said, gesturing towards the ceiling.

"You mean to Maureen?"

"Maureen, Gary, all of the executives and vice-presidents and other directors and managers," he replied.

"I'm working on that too," she said. "Are you asking if you can help?"

Ravi nodded as if his question had been obvious.

"Think about how moving it will be when people visit the marketing department, and they feel the difference," Jess said. "You can help by developing the skills in yourself and spreading them to the people you work with. Once we have enough people on our team using the skills, I'm sure the other VPs and Gary will be coming to ask us what we've been doing differently."

Ravi's chest was puffing out, as if he was taking a deep breath. Jessica wouldn't have been surprised if he ripped open his buttoned shirt to reveal a superhero emblem.

"Sounds like a plan," he said.

"Are you ready to be the leader that drives change?"

Ravi hopped up, his chair nearly toppling over.

"I am," he said.

"Then get to work," she said.

Watching her shining soldier hustle out of her office, armed for battle with tools he would continue to develop for himself, Jessica felt whole and complete.

21

FRESH START

Jessica took a sip of coffee as she waited for Maureen to review the document.

"This is it?" Maureen asked.

"It's a start," Jessica replied. "It's already growing organically. People like Ravi are contributing their insights."

Maureen hadn't looked up since being handed the folder, something Jessica would have judged her for in the past. In the present, Jessica wanted Maureen's critical eye, so she remained patiently still. She was no longer making up stories to justify her manager's actions.

"Where did you get all this?" Maureen asked once she had finished. She dropped the document on the desk, looking up at Jessica.

"From the depths of my imagination," Jessica said with a smile. "It struck me that in creating a plan about people and how we work, live, and play together, it should not be a typical plan with *what* to do and *when* to do it by. But rather more about *who* we're enrolling and *how* we're equipping them. And I wanted to keep this simple. The skills are practical and easy to use. That's how we'll keep finding ways to do less, accomplish more, and make a difference."

Maureen raised one of her eyebrows at Jessica.

"That's the whole point, isn't it?"

Maureen's eyes drifted back to the document on the desk.

"How can I help?" she asked, tapping it with her finger.

This simple question signified such a massive change in their working relationship. Before, Maureen might have hijacked or torpedoed the project. Now, she was asking for guidance and leadership, offering her insights for the betterment of the cause.

"Let's put our money where our mouths are," Jessica said. "Getting you on board and developing these skills in you will do a lot to help this culture spread throughout the company."

The intensity in Maureen's eyes was enough to melt steel, as it always was when a new challenge confronted her. The difference was that she was willing to work with her team, instead of feeling the need to command their every move.

Maureen slowly reached out and picked up the culture document again, a quiver of the pages betraying a slight shake of her hand.

"Jessica, I want to acknowledge you," she said. "You've accomplished a breakthrough with yourself and this team."

It was clunky, not yet natural.

"You've developed and documented these skill sets for us and have implemented them into the way you interact with the rest of the team and me. You've pushed us to change our culture and have shown perseverance, dedication, and compassion throughout."

It was like watching a child ride her bike without training wheels for the first time. She started a bit wobbly but began to gain control as she pushed forward.

"You've overcome all of our doubts that anything could change, and your self-doubt too, I'm sure. You've taken on this entire team and our work culture on your own, and you've ignited change in a way that no one could have imagined possible."

Maureen lifted her head. Sheepish was an odd look on her.

"How did I do?" she asked.

"Perfect," Jessica said. "Thank you for your acknowledgment."

It felt like Jessica was sipping on a hot tea, warmth spreading through her insides and out to her extremities.

"What are you experiencing right now?" she asked Maureen.

"It's kind of tingly and warm. I don't know why I was so nervous."

"It gets easier every time," Jessica replied.

Maureen inclined her head, indicating that she understood.

"And how about you?" Jessica said. "What's the impact on you?"

"I feel stronger," she said. "Like I can accomplish anything. It's almost like…"

"Like the parched earth is a little less dry?"

Maureen smiled.

"Yes, like the parched earth is a little less dry. A lot less, actually. It's almost ready to be turned and tilled, for the seeds to be planted."

"Then let's see what kind of ideas we can plant in there," Jessica said. "And what grows out of them."

Jessica sensed that there was something Maureen wasn't saying, so she waited for her boss to speak.

"Do you think you could help me apply these skills to my relationship with Gary?" Maureen asked.

"I would be happy to," Jessica replied, smiling. Receiving a request for help from her boss was an enormous and exciting transformation. This promised a remarkable impact for everyone involved. Yet Maureen still seemed to be lost in thought.

"I want to share something with you," she finally said. "Something no one knows about me."

"Please," Jessica gestured for her to continue.

"When I first moved here, I changed my name. It's common practice for immigrants to do this; it helps make the cultural transition a bit easier, especially when I immigrated. Maureen is my chosen name, but my given name is Amoy. It means 'beautiful goddess' back home, but I so desperately wanted to fit in when I moved here that I decided to change it."

There was a warmth in the room, as if they were sitting around a campfire.

"I'm honored," Jessica said. "Can I ask why you shared that with me?"

"Because I want a fresh start," Amoy replied. "I'm ready for people to learn about who I really am instead of who I've had to be at work. I chose to forget the ambitious vision I had for this team when I first took the job. It seemed less and less possible every day, so I chose instead to be someone who controls, instructs, and manages my people. I finally feel like I'm ready to unlearn that harmful behavior. You've helped me realize that my dreams and goals are within *my* grasp."

Jessica stood up and reached across the table, extending her hand to shake Amoy's as if it was their first time meeting.

"It's a pleasure to meet you, Amoy," she said. "I'm Jess."

Amoy leaped up, clearing the lump in her throat and clasping Jess's hand with pride.

"Hello Jess, it's a pleasure to meet you too."

Belief Shift: Manager mindset (which stems from how your job performance is evaluated) is about doing your job well, including making sure each person on your staff meets their own performance metrics. Leaders accept that individual performance matters, but also understand that difference-making comes when everyone on the team works and plays extraordinarily well together.

DAKOTA LAMARRE

• STAGE 5 •

GREAT LEADER, GREAT HUMAN BEING

22

ON THE OTHER SIDE

They strode in unison through the rows of cubicles, Jessica's feet clad in fashionable black pumps, Maureen's in professional blue flats.

Since Jessica had first presented her culture document and skills matrix to Maureen several months ago, they had made these Friday afternoon walkabouts a habit. Their attention to doing less to accomplish more made for more manageable schedules, so they could make a difference by, for example, taking an informal pulse on team morale and engagement.

They now attended meetings to get updates and work on big-picture brainstorming, bringing different perspectives and challenging their team members to get the best out of them. The days of delegating and continually checking in, following up, second requesting, and reprimanding were coming to an end.

Previously, they needed divine intervention just to catch up. Now, it took an act of God for their team to fall seriously behind. People solved their problems and set their schedules, sharing ideas and firing on all cylinders more often than not. They didn't need to be "managed." They showed up and did their best work.

It wasn't yet ideal, and the transition hadn't been seamless. An initial wave of confusion was echoed by a smaller wave of resistance, as people gradually came to understand that the beliefs they clung to about managing and working with people no longer served them. A few on the marketing team chose to leave, but the team's new culture enabled them to fill the vacant positions with star players whose personal values already aligned with those of the team. Their new culture was going viral.

The atmosphere was relaxed, a complete shift from before. The workload was still considerable, and there was just as much to accomplish as before, but the hectic habit of always "doing" more was gone. There was more openness in conversations, signaling trust and acceptance. They were acknowledged regularly and celebrated vigorously. Where once the air was thick with tension and confusion, people were now calm and cool. Small groups frequently formed; naturally, the discussions were focused on work, but often erupted into bouts of laughter.

As one such example presented itself, a small huddle bursting into hysterics, Jessica and Maureen saw a young woman break off from the group to make a mark on a whiteboard mounted on the wall. Taking Ravi's input, Jessica had insisted on creating this custom whiteboard, which measured things like "belly laughs." Along the top ran the words **I Win Only When We All Win.**

People from other teams visited the marketing department as much as possible, often for more than just business purposes. Many couldn't pinpoint why they loved visiting, but found themselves returning to their teams appreciated, challenged to do their best, and coached to solve their problems. Most of them left enlightened with an explanation of the skills that had just been used on them. Many of them were enrolled to learn how to apply the skills themselves. The skills matrix Jessica had created had since been refined and adopted by her team, and the results indicated that their fresh culture was infectious.

As Jessica and Maureen rounded a corner, the conference room came into view. Through the glass wall, they saw Ravi watching proudly as one of his team members led the meeting. He saw them and flashed a giant grin and a thumbs up. Maureen was smiling, something she had been doing a lot lately.

Ravi's customer database re-segmentation project made such an impact that they named him the project head and assigned him a group to oversee. With his team assembled around him now, it was easy to tell that they were engaged and contributing to the cause, using the skills that Ravi had laid down as the foundation of their team's culture. Ravi was more like an orchestra conductor than a manager, pointing to people in succession as they chimed in with ways to build on each others' ideas.

"*That's what I call a win*," said the voice in Jessica's head. Her inner dialogue was increasingly less aggressive these days.

The usual industry and competitive pressures facing their company hadn't disappeared. If anything, they were more intense than ever, but their team could handle them, collaborating more effectively to generate insights and make better decisions faster. They were doing things right the first time and executing quickly without fear of making mistakes.

They still had their blunders but didn't waste time dwelling on them. When Jessica implemented the A-squared, C-squared principle with her entire team, she saw her people start acknowledging each other even for their mistakes as a way to spotlight and showcase what worked. They took the learnings and pivoted faster and more effectively.

Arriving back in Maureen's office at the end of their walkthrough, Jessica took a seat in front of the desk to finish their debrief.

"You sure you're going to be okay without me?" Maureen asked. For the first time in a decade, she was going to visit her home country. It was a joy for Jess to see her new friend, Amoy, not only taking a break, but reconnecting with herself, her past, and her culture.

"We'll be fine," Jess said and meant it.

"I was only joking," Amoy smiled. "I have total confidence in you all."

"Have fun," Jess stopped in the doorway on her way out of Amoy's office. "And remember, you're only allowed to check your emails once a day while you're away."

"I'll only answer if I'm asked something directly," Amoy replied.

"I promise you won't be. We've got this, Amoy," Jess said with a wink.

Jessica glowed with joy for her friend as she walked back to her own office.

Later that day, there was a knock at Jessica's door. The man in the dark suit and red tie limped in, somehow looking older and younger at the same time.

"Jessica?" Gary said. "I wanted to stop by and commend you on what you've been doing with your team. Maureen showed me everything and spoke very highly of your work and the initiative you've taken."

"Thank you, Gary," she said. "I appreciate your acknowledgment."

"I'm wondering why you didn't share your work with us on your own," Gary pressed on. "I thought it was your initiative."

"Maureen and I decided that she didn't need my help to share all this with you and the rest of the executive team," Jessica replied. "Keeping two people from doing one person's job is one way we do less and accomplish more. That's the beauty of this work, Gary. I've taught Maureen the skills, and she's shifted her beliefs to the point that I have complete confidence in her ability to share them with others."

"She's been using those skills with me," he said with pride. He tried to puff his chest out but groaned in pain. "And I think it's working."

This was how Jessica saw success in her work, the difference someone had made in another person's life using the skills she had developed after shifting her beliefs. She was excited for the opportunity Maureen had created for Gary, for the journey he was embarking upon, and the bright future awaiting him with each step.

"This is just the tip of the iceberg," Jessica replied. "The few skills I shared were enough to create a change around here, but you should see what's coming next. People are working together to co-create more skills of their own, testing them, documenting them, and sharing them. It's already grown quite a bit bigger than just Maureen and me."

Gary nodded, clearly intrigued, then clasped the back of his neck.

"You alright, boss?" Jessica asked, eyeing him with concern. "You look like you're hurting."

"I bit the bullet and started working with a personal trainer," he replied. "The guy has been putting me through the ringer."

Though his belly wasn't yet gone, nor were the issues facing their company, Gary was showing signs of his old self again.

"This old bag of bones isn't what it used to be," he said to Jessica with a twinkle in his eye. "Anyways, just thought I'd come down to say thank you. Keep up the good work."

Jessica smiled as her company president walked out of her office, steadying his sore body by placing a hand on the doorframe.

"I think there's some Aspirin in the kitchen," she called after him.

"Thank you!" he called back. Jessica could tell from his tone that he was also smiling.

Jessica looked up from her desk to gaze, like a proud parent, over her team. She felt the buzz of positive energy, accomplishment, and success. That was what she had always wanted.

"*Congratulations*," said her inner voice. "*This is what you've been picturing ever since you became a manager.*"

She chuckled to herself.

"*I've promoted myself*," Jessica replied internally. "*I'm done being just a manager. Now I'm a leader too.*"

Jessica knew this was not the time to take their foot off the gas, despite the successes her team was enjoying. There would still be setbacks and obstacles to overcome. She had faith in her team and their ability to stick together and remain human in the face of both success and adversity.

Smiling, she took a deep breath, then turned to smile at her family photo from Greece. She was at peace.

23

WELCOME HOME

Walking through the front door, Jess smelled chili powder and cumin. Paul must have already started cooking the ground beef for dinner. A tiny figure came rocketing around the corner. Lily jumped up into Jess's arms, ecstatic to see her mom.

"Mommy!" Lily shrieked with delight. "I already finished all my homework for the entire weekend."

"That's wonderful, my darling," Jess said, putting her daughter and her bag down on the ground. "I acknowledge you for getting your homework done tonight. You showed focus and perseverance. How do you want to celebrate?"

"Nachos and a movie!" she laughed, sprinting back to the kitchen.

Jess could hear her daughter and husband from the other room.

"She's home, she's home!" Lily exclaimed.

"She is?" Paul said, joking with his child. "I didn't hear her. Are you sure?"

"She is, Dad! I just saw her."

"You'd better bring her a cocktail then," Paul said.

A commotion of tinkling and the sound of a drink being poured brought a smile to Jess's face as she hung up her coat. Lily appeared in the hallway again, much slower this time, her tongue out in intense concentration as she carried a glass full to the brim with muddled strawberries, mint, and bubbly water.

Paul trailed behind her, looking sexy in his apron. Jess gave him a look of approval after taking a sip of the beverage. He planted a kiss on her cheek and a hand on the small of her back, guiding her towards the kitchen.

"Mine has vodka in it," he winked, pointing towards his drink on the counter.

"None for me, thanks," she said, her hand naturally finding her belly.

Work no longer followed her home. Any work-related discussion with Paul was about sharing and celebrating, not sulking and complaining. Not only was she afforded more time to spend with her family, she wasn't as distracted or stressed when she wasn't at the office. As had been her intention, she made it to soccer games and dance recitals, to dinners and movie nights, even scheduling regular date nights with Paul.

"Mommy, is Auntie Amoy coming over for dinner tonight?"

Maureen had been coming over for dinner about once a month, Ravi sometimes joining them as well. In professional settings, they were still Maureen and Jessica, boss and employee on an increasingly productive team. However, outside the office and in moments that called for them to draw upon their humanity, they were Amoy and Jess, friends enjoying life together and supporting one another.

"No, sweetie," Jess replied. "She's going on vacation, remember."

"Oh, I forgot," Lily said, unfazed by her mistake.

Jess was constantly impressed by how much of a role model her daughter already was. She and Paul were creating an environment that supported Lily to grow into a great leader, which is to say, a great human being. They had used Jess's culture contract and skills matrix as a template to design something similar at home, having weekly family meetings to celebrate and acknowledge their accomplishments and to be present and communicate with each other. Jess and Paul also had their own meetings where they talked about how they would parent Lily and make time for romance in their relationship.

Jess scanned the whiteboard that now took up a sizable section of their refrigerator door. There were areas where they could record the number of acknowledgments given each week or the number of hours spent on their hobbies. There was also a section that measured how many times Jess made it home in time for dinner.

"I can't wait to see grandma and grandpa," Lily piped up again.

She was referring to the vacation they had booked, a late run to their family cottage to visit Jess's parents before they closed it for the season. They were all excited for their first getaway together in years, and Jess was excited to take a full week off work without having to worry about the office imploding.

As they sat down at the dinner table, Jess peered into the sunroom where she had set up her easel in a makeshift painting studio. The hours she spent painting was one of her success metrics. She found that when she spent at least an hour working on her art each week, her spirit felt nourished, and her creativity flowed more easily in all aspects of her life. It was gratifying to be speaking through art again.

In the corner of the sunroom, Jess had hung a print she had bought from the gift shop at the art gallery. She had insisted on taking Paul and Lily, introducing her daughter to some of her favorite works, and walking out with a print of *Automat*. Every once in a while, Jess could swear the woman in the painting took a sip of coffee or shifted in her seat. Probably just her imagination. Either way, she took these as signs that her friend was always with her in spirit, and she found comfort in the thought that neither of them had to be lonely anymore.

Together they finished eating, and everyone helped clear the table, do the dishes, and clean the kitchen. They worked as a cohesive unit, and in no time they were sitting down in front of the TV. Jess allowed herself a deep breath as Paul helped Lily pick out a movie. It was the kind of stress-free breath that came from a deep-seated sense of peace.

Their family was firing on all cylinders, much like her team at the office. Jess felt connected to them as a real person, instead of just a provider or a late-night scavenger rummaging through leftovers. In the space created since she had taken control of her destiny at work, they had let their love bring them together as a connected, unified team. This was her most noteworthy reward for all her bravery and perseverance. She had gotten her family back.

...

Everyone was cuddled together on the couch, Jess leaning on Paul's shoulder, their daughter curled up asleep between them. Even though it was past her bedtime, neither of them could bring themselves to move Lily upstairs.

Jess was tired, not from stress or from doing too much, but from accomplishment, from making a difference regularly and often. Paul looked over at her.

"What is it?" she asked.

"I'm happy to have you back," he whispered. It was clear that he was referring to much more than Jess being home from work on time.

He placed his hand on top of hers, on the small bump that was already forming at Jess's midsection. Their renewed quality time and their invigorated relationship had produced a new addition to their family, set to arrive in just over six months.

As Jess gazed into Paul's eyes, gone was the doubt about having another child, that her work would keep her from being a good mother or wife, and that her life was somehow outside of her control. Now, she doubted nothing, knowing that she had found her path.

She started each day excited to be a mother, a wife, a friend, and a great leader. She had learned to see the difference she was making in the lives of those around her, and the impact those people were making in the lives of those around them.

Jess looked through Paul's office doorway, where they had started work on their project together. Combining Jess's skills and belief shifts with Paul's writing ability, they had already made solid progress on writing a book that would tell her story and share her skills with many more people than she could ever have hoped to interact with directly. It was their mission to share with the world how possible it was to create change from anywhere.

Paul had already spoken to some of his connections in the publishing industry, and it appeared likely that her ideas would get out into the world. It could be bigger than a case study for MBA students or something to help just her company. It could create a revolution that could spread around the globe.

This was her purpose, to make that difference for herself, her family, her colleagues, and the world. This was what she had wanted since first stepping into a leadership role.

She couldn't wait to get back to work on Monday.

Belief Shift: Most employees started life as people, and they remain people to this day. Managers obsess over getting work done right, hitting goals and targets. Leaders have a different lens, one that appreciates each person as a unique human being with hopes, fears, dreams, ambitions, obstacles, emotions, and lives. Leaders are authentic and know that being themselves inspires authenticity and excellence in others.

AFTERWORD

What if this story weren't fiction?
    Human beings have been telling stories to share information for thousands of years. Like fables from a forgotten age, this story contains valuable messages of practical truth such as:

- YOU are the solution.
- YOU can transform your relationships and environment and create meaningful change from anywhere.
- YOU can do less, accomplish more, and make a difference at work and in your life.
- YOU have the power to create a transformational culture shift.

It's About You

You might be saying, "Yes, but my situation, my stressors, and the people I have to work with aren't like those in your story."

It's not about your situation, your stressors, or the people around you. It's about YOU. As we saw with Jessica, it wasn't merely her ability to learn new skills or even to shift her beliefs, it was her actions that created change. So we ask you, what will you do with what you now know?

"Happily ever after" is an outcome we want you to experience. We want you to (re)discover the joy, fulfillment, and meaning in your work. We want you to achieve your ambitions without sacrificing your family or well-being. Instead of merely coping with "the way it is," we want to equip you to navigate, climb, and ultimately shape the world in which you work, live, and play.

In the world of work, we (managers especially) obsess with "it." This includes tasks, strategy, plans, targets, processes, issues, rules, and technology. If you're anything like Jessica, you're probably really good at "it" work. Perhaps the most important theme of our story is that focusing on the "who" is what really makes a difference.

We contend it's not about "it," but about "who." It's not about "managing," but about "leading." Regardless of where you are in your company hierarchy, we hope you now believe you can make a difference and are inspired to do so.

GEORGE ANASTASOPOULOS

Find out more and start your journey now by visiting www.leadershipfundamentals.com/ilm. The answers to any questions you might have, and everything you need to get started, are there.

ACKNOWLEDGMENTS

As seen in this story, acknowledgments are an important part of this book and the methodologies of Leadership Fundamentals.

From George

Acknowledgments to my wife for enduring more than 40 years of our marriage, for being the most non-judgmental person who's ever lived, who did the heavy lifting (although you never saw it that way) of raising three amazing daughters while I worked late and was rarely around, who accepted me for who I am (warts and all), and who taught me to be a human being by being the best example of one I can ever find.

Acknowledgments to my daughters for learning from your mother the values of love, caring, and compassion. Thank you for your intense dedication to your passions in life and for the generosity you regularly show in patiently and lovingly accepting me as I am.

From Dakota

This book could not have been written without the support of my family, both given and chosen. It would take a lot more pages to list the many people who have contributed to my life.

You know who you are, and I'm grateful to you for helping, tolerating, questioning, feeding, sheltering, pushing, empowering, inspiring, and believing in me. This book is the beginning of me giving back to all of you and many others. Thank you for your support. I love you all.

From Us

We acknowledge you, our reader, for having already accomplished something meaningful. You read this book hoping it contained value and wisdom.

Your curiosity, commitment, and steadfast belief that you have the power to create real and lasting change will define you as a leader. Reading this book may be your first, next, or final step to overcoming the challenges facing all managers today—making a difference in the lives of the people around you, including, and especially, your own.

If these messages resonate with you and you're motivated to take action from them, you are a leader, and this book was written for you. Thank you.

DAKOTA LAMARRE

GEORGE ANASTASOPOULOS

George Anastasopoulos, Founder and Head Coach at Leadership Fundamentals Inc. is a Professional Certified Coach (PCC) with the International Coaching Federation (ICF), who uses insightful, practical, and fun approaches to transform managers into leaders. A former corporate manager, executive, and leader for 20 years, George grew tired of "the way it is" and dedicated himself to leadership training and coaching. A passionate storyteller, he creates simple, unorthodox, yet highly effective ways for humans to work, play, and live together. Whether at work or play, you're guaranteed to experience passion, energy, and laughter with George.

DAKOTA LAMARRE

Dakota LaMarre is a young author with a penchant for business and storytelling. Fueled by the belief that crafting stories is one of the most challenging and important things that humans do, he is committed to seeking out brilliant leaders, working with them to co-create stories that bring their ideas to the people that can benefit the most. When he's not out hiking, jamming on his guitar, or bothering his cat, he's on a mission to create books and other content that empowers professionals to take back control of their careers and lives.

LOVING MONDAYS GOES VIRAL!

Love the book? Here's how you can help make loving Mondays go viral:

- **Make it happen** – use the skills, create a culture shift at your workplace, and live a life of loving Mondays (and every other day)!
- **Share with a friend** – recommend the book, or better yet, get them their own copy!
- **Leave a review** – whether on Amazon, Goodreads, Google, Apple, or your favorite retailer's website. We really appreciate you taking the time to leave one!
- **Get social** – talk about the book on your favorite social media platforms, tell your friends and followers what you loved about it, and what you hope they can gain from reading it!
- **Reach out to us** – whether it's through social media, email, our websites, or by phone, we love having conversations with amazing people!
- Please contact us for **speaking engagements**, **press and media inquiries**, and **volume discounts**.

Find out more and start your own journey by visiting leadershipfundamentals.com or contact me directly using the following information to explore how we can work together to make loving Mondays go viral!

Dakota LaMarre
1 (905) 732-8754
inquiry@dakotalamarre.com

Printed in Canada